WHAT HAPPENS AFTER DEATH? BUDDHA ANSWERS

FROM THE PALI CANON

*A translation into English
from the Sinhala translation
by Ven. Kiribathgoda Gnānānanda Thero.*

A Mahamegha Publication

WHAT HAPPENS AFTER DEATH?

BUDDHA ANSWERS

FROM THE PALI CANON

Ven. Kiribathgoda Gnānānanda Thero

ISBN : 978-955-687-113-5

<u>Computer Typesetting by</u>

Buddha Meditation Centre
Markham, Ontario, Canada L6C 1P2
Telephone: 905-927-7117
www.meditationgta.org

<u>Published by</u>

Mahamegha Publishers
Waduwawa, Yatigaloluwa, Polgahawela, Sri Lanka.
Telephone: +94 37 2053300 I 76 8255703
www.mahamevnawa.lk
mahameghapublishers@gmail.com

*Namo Tassa Bhagavato Arahato
Sammā Sambuddhassa!*

*Homage to the Blessed One, the Worthy One,
the Supremely Enlightened One!*

Contents

Chapter Five: Goal of Human Life

Introduction

Dear Sons, Daughters, and Devotees,

We are very fortunate to learn about the kinds of knowledge of the Supreme Buddha. Our great teacher, the Supreme Buddha, had an extraordinary knowledge to see past lives of beings. In the Bhayaberava Sutta, the Buddha tells us how he gained the knowledge to see his own past lives:

"When my mind was concentrated, purified, bright, clear, free from defilements, open, soft, steady, and unshakeable, I directed my mind to the knowledge of recollecting my past lives. I recollected my various past lives, that is, one birth, two... five, ten... fifty, a hundred, a thousand, a hundred thousand, many eons of the cycle of formation and destruction of this earth. In one life I had such a name, belonged to such a clan, had such an appearance. Such was my food, such my experience of pleasure and pain, and such the end of my life. Passing away from that life, I was reborn in another place. There too I had such a name, belonged to such a clan, had such an appearance. Such was my food, such my experience of pleasure and pain, and such the end of my life. Passing away from that state, I was reborn here. I remembered my different past lives in every detail. This was the first knowledge I attained in the first watch of the night. My ignorance was destroyed, knowledge arose, darkness was destroyed, and light arose. All of which happens when one is mindful, passionate, and firm."

Next, the Supreme Buddha gained the knowledge to see how other beings travel in this cycle of samsara, one life to another, because of their good and bad actions.

"When my mind was concentrated, purified, bright, clear, free from defilements, open, soft, steady, and unshakeable, I directed it to gain the knowledge of the passing away and rebirth of beings. With my divine eye, which is purified and surpassing the human eye, I saw beings' passing away and rebirth, and I discovered how they are inferior and superior, beautiful and ugly, and fortunate and unfortunate in accordance with their kamma: beings who committed bad actions by body, speech, and mind, who insulted enlightened ones, held wrong views, and did bad deeds, with the break-up of their body, after death, have been reborn in a bad destination, the lower realms, in hell. But, those beings who committed good deeds with body, speech, and mind, who did not insult enlightened ones, who held right views, and did good deeds, with the break-up of the body, after death, have been reborn in the good destinations, in the heavenly world. Therefore, with the use of my divine eye, which is purified and surpassing the human eye, I saw passing away and rebirth of beings, and I discovered how they are inferior and superior, beautiful and ugly, and fortunate and unfortunate in accordance with their kamma."

Finally, in the third watch of the night, Supreme Buddha realized the true nature of the life and escaped from the cycle of rebirth.

"When my concentrated mind was purified, bright, unblemished, rid of imperfection, malleable, uncomplicated, steady, and calm, I directed it to the knowledge of the destruction of taints. I directly knew as it actually is 'This is suffering, this is the origin of suffering, this is the cessation of suffering, and this is the way leading to cessation of suffering.' I directly knew as it actually is 'These are the taints, this is the origin of taints, this is the cessation of the taints, and this the way leading to the cessation of taints."

"When I knew and saw thus, my mind was liberated from the taint of sensual desire, from the taint of existence, and from the taint of ignorance. When it was liberated, there came the knowledge 'It is liberated.' I directly knew 'Birth is destroyed, the holy life has been lived, what had to be done has been done, and there is no more coming to any state of existence.' "This was the third true knowledge attained by me in the last watch of the night. Ignorance was banished and true knowledge arose, darkness was banished and light arose, as it happens in one who abides diligently, ardently, and resolutely."

The Supreme Buddha is the knower of all worlds. He knows the qualities of all the worlds and the way beings are born in these different worlds as he explains in the Maha Sihanada Sutta:

"Sariputta, there are five types of beings. What are the five? Hell beings, animals, ghosts, human beings, and gods.

I understand hell, and the path and way leading to hell. I also understand how one who has entered this path will, on the breaking up of the body, after death, reappear as a hell being.

I understand the animal world, and the path and way leading to the animal world. I also understand how one who has entered this path will, on the breaking up of the body, after death, be reborn as an animal.

I understand the realm of ghosts, and the path and way leading to the realm of ghosts. I also understand how one who has entered this path will, on the breaking up of the body, after death, reappear in the realm of ghosts.

I understand human beings, and the path and way leading to the human world. I also understand how one who has entered this path will, on the breaking up of the body, after death, reappear among human beings.

I understand the gods, and the path and way leading to the world of the gods. I also understand how one who has entered this path will, on the breaking up of the body, after death, reappear in a happy destination, in the heavenly world."

Most fortunately, Noble Disciples have the opportunity to escape from all worlds by attaining Nibbana. The Supreme Buddha is the only teacher to show the way to Nibbana.

"I understand Nibbana and the path and way leading to Nibbana. I also understand how one who has entered this path will, by realizing it for himself with direct knowledge, here and now, enter upon and abide in the liberation of the mind and liberation by wisdom that is taintless with the destruction of the taints."

From this book, you are going to learn the actions that lead to the bad worlds and how beings are suffering in those worlds. You will notice that they all lived in the human world like we do now. Here, the Supreme Buddha explains the suffering of those worlds with these similes:

"Sariputta by encompassing mind with mind, I understand a person by his very nature: 'This person behaves as such, conducts himself as such, and has taken such a path that on the dissolution of the body, after death, he will reappear in a plane of misery, in an unhappy destination, in the worst destination, in hell.' Then, with the divine eye, which is purified and surpasses the human, I see that on the dissolution of the body, after death, he has reappeared in a plane of misery, in an unhappy destination, in the worst destination, in hell, and is experiencing extremely painful, racking, and piercing feelings. Suppose there was a charcoal pit deeper than a man's height, full of glowing coals without flame or smoke. Then, a man scorched and exhausted by hot weather, weary, parched, and thirsty came by a path going in only one way and directed to that same charcoal pit. Then, a man with good sight on seeing him would say 'This person behaves as such, conducts himself as such, and has taken such a path that he will come to this same charcoal pit', and later on, he sees that he has fallen into that charcoal pit and is experiencing extremely painful, racking, and piercing feelings. So, too, by encompassing mind with mind... piercing feelings."

"By encompassing mind with mind, I understand a person by his very nature: 'This person behaves as such, conducts himself as such, and has taken such a path that on the dissolution of the body, after death, he will reappear in the animal realm.' Then, with the divine eye, which is purified and surpasses the human, I see that on the dissolution of the body, after death, he has reappeared in the animal realm and is experiencing strong painful, racking, and piercing feelings. Suppose there was a cesspit deeper than a man's height, full of filth. Then, a man scorched and exhausted by hot weather, weary, parched, and thirsty came by a path going in only one way and directed to that same cesspit. Then, a man with good sight on seeing him would say 'This person behaves as such... that he will come to this same cesspit', and later on, he sees that he has fallen into that cesspit and is experiencing strong painful, racking, and piercing feelings. So, too, by encompassing mind with mind... piercing feelings."

"By encompassing mind with mind, I understand a person by his very nature: 'This person behaves as such, conducts himself as such, and has taken such a path that on the dissolution of the body, after death, he will reappear in the realm of ghosts.' Then, with the divine eye... I see that... he has reappeared in the realm of ghosts and is experiencing very painful feelings. Suppose there was a tree growing on uneven ground with scanty foliage casting a dappled shade. Then, a man scorched and exhausted by hot weather, weary, parched, and thirsty came by a path going in only one way and directed to that same tree. Then, a man with good sight on seeing him would say 'This person behaves as such... that he will come to this same tree', and later on, he sees that he is sitting or lying in the shade of that tree experiencing a very painful feelings. So, too, by encompassing mind with mind... very painful feelings."

"By encompassing mind with mind, I understand a person by his very nature: 'This person behaves as such, conducts himself as such, and has taken such a path that on the dissolution of the body, after death, he will reappear among human beings.' Then, with the divine eye...... I see that... he has reappeared among human beings and is experiencing pleasant feelings. Suppose there was a tree growing on even ground with thick foliage casting a deep shade. Then, a man scorched and exhausted by hot weather, weary, parched, and thirsty came by a path going in only one way and directed to that same tree. Then, a man with good sight on seeing him would say 'This person behaves as such... that he will come to this same tree', and later on, he sees that he is sitting or lying in the shade of that tree experiencing pleasant feelings. So, too, by encompassing mind with mind... pleasant feelings."

"By encompassing mind with mind, I understand a person by his very nature: 'This person behaves as such, conducts himself as such, and has taken such a path that on the dissolution of the body, after death, he will reappear in a happy destination, in the heavenly world.' Then, with the divine eye... I see that... he has reappeared in a happy destination, in the heavenly world and is experiencing extremely pleasant feelings. Suppose there was a mansion, and it had an upper chamber plastered within and without, shut off, secured by bars, with shuttered windows, and in it there was a couch spread with rugs, blankets, and sheets, with a deerskin coverlet, with a canopy as well as crimson pillows for both (head and feet). Then, a man scorched and exhausted by hot weather, weary, parched, and thirsty came by a path going in only one way and directed to that same mansion. Then, a man with good sight on seeing him would say 'This person behaves as such... that he will come to this same mansion', and later on, he sees that he is sitting or lying in that upper chamber in that mansion experiencing extremely pleasant feelings. So, too, by encompassing mind with mind... extremely pleasant feelings."

"By encompassing mind with mind, I understand a person by his very nature: 'This person behaves as such, conducts himself as such, and has taken such a path that by realizing it for himself with direct knowledge, he, here and now, will enter upon and abide in the deliverance of mind and deliverance by wisdom that is taintless with the destruction of the taints.' Later on, I see that by realizing it for himself with direct knowledge, he, here and now, enters upon and abides in the deliverance of mind and deliverance by wisdom that is taintless with the destruction of the taints, and is experiencing extremely pleasant feelings. Suppose there was a pond with clean, agreeable, cool water, transparent, with smooth banks, delightful, and nearby a dense wood. Then, a man scorched and exhausted by hot weather, weary, parched, and thirsty came by a path going in only one way and directed towards that same pond. Then, a man with good sight on seeing him would say 'This person behaves as such... that he will come to this same pond', and, later on, he sees that he has plunged into the pond, bathed, drunk, and relieved all his distress, fatigue, and fever and has come out again and is sitting or lying in the wood experiencing extremely pleasant feelings. So, too, by encompassing mind with mind... extremely pleasant feelings. Sariputta, these are the five destinations."

Dear children, parents, and Dhamma friends, read these discourses very carefully. May the teachings of the Buddha help you to develop a fear of doing wrong actions in your precious human life. May you practice generosity. May you keep the precepts well. May you control your bad thoughts. By practicing Dhamma, may you escape from rebirth in bad worlds.

May all of you realize The Four Noble Truths in this Gautama Buddha's Dispensation.

With Metta,
Ven. Kiribathgoda Gnānānanda Thera
Mahamevnawa Monastery,
Waduwawa, Yatigal-oluwa, Polgahawela,
Sri Lanka.

2556 Buddhist Years/ 2016

Chapter One: Hell

1.1 Bālapandita Suttaṁ—The Fool and The Wise

This is as I heard: One day, the Blessed One was living in the city of Sāvatthi, at Jeta's park in Anāthapindika's monastery. The Blessed One addressed the monks saying, "Monks." "Bhante" they replied. Then, the Blessed One taught this discourse:

"Monks, there are three characteristics of a fool, signs of a fool, and features of a fool. What are the three? A fool thinks bad thoughts, speaks bad words, and does bad deeds. If a fool weren't so, how would the wise know him thus: 'This person is a fool, an inferior man?' But, because a fool is one who thinks bad thoughts, speaks bad words, and does bad deeds, thus, the wise know him as: 'This man is a fool, an inferior man'"

"A fool feels pain and grief here and now in three ways. Suppose a fool is seated in an assembly or in a street, or at an intersection, and people there are discussing matters that are related to evil actions done by others, and if the fool is one who kills beings, steals, commits sexual misconduct, lies, or takes intoxicating drinks and drugs, he thinks: ' These people here are discussing matters related to evil actions; these evil actions are found in me and I am doing these evil actions.' This is the first type of pain and grief that a fool feels here and now."

"Again, when a robber is caught, a fool sees that kings give him many kinds of tortures: having him beaten with whips, beaten with canes, beaten with clubs; having his hands cut off, his feet cut off, his hands and feet cut off, his ears cut off, his nose cut off, his ears and his nose cut off; having his head smashed; having his head shaved with gravel until the skull is visible; having his mouth opened with an iron hook and with a fire torch placed in it, having his body wrapped with oily clothes, and then set fire on the clothes, having his arms wrapped with oily clothes and then set fire on the clothes, having his skin removed from his neck downwards and dragged, having his skin removed from his neck downwards and from his feet upwards and tied them together, having put spikes through two knees and two elbows to the ground and set fire to the body, having his body stabbed with hooks and smashed flesh, having his entire flesh torn into small pieces, having his entire body jabbed with holes and having applied boiling oil into them, having him on his side and a spike drilled through his ears to the ground then by holding his legs they spin him on the spot, having his bones broken into small pieces with stones, having him splashed with boiling oil, having him thrown to be devoured by dogs, being alive he is speared with spikes, and having his head cut off with a sword. Seeing these he thinks: 'These evil actions are found in me and I am doing these evil actions.' This is the second type of pain and grief that a fool feels here and now."

"Again, when a fool is on his chair or on his bed, or resting on the ground, then the evil actions that he did in the past by body, speech and mind cover him, overspread him, and envelope him. Just as the shadow of a great mountain peak in the evening covers, overspreads, and envelopes the earth, so too, when a fool is on his chair or on his bed or resting on the ground, the evil actions that he did in the past by body, speech and mind cover him, overspread him, and envelope him. Then, the fool thinks: 'I have not done what is good; I have not done what is wholesome; and I have not made myself a refuge for fear. I have done what is evil; I have done what is cruel; and I have done what is wicked. When I pass away, I will be reborn where beings who have done evil are born.' He sorrows, grieves, laments, and weeps beating his chest and loses mindfulness. This is the third type of pain and grief that a fool feels here and now."

"Monks, a fool, having committed bad actions by body, speech, and mind, at the break-up of the body after death, is reborn in the plane of misery - in the worst destination: in hell."

(HELL)

"If one were to describe suffering anywhere to be extremely displeasing, extremely disagreeable, and extremely unappealing, it is the suffering in Hell that should be described so. It is very hard to explain the suffering in hell even with a simile."

When this was said, a monk asked the Blessed One: "Please Bhante, can a simile be given?"

"Yes, a simile can be given." The Blessed One said: "Monks, say there was a robber that was caught and presented to the king, saying: 'Sire, here is a robber, command punishment to him as you wish.' Then, the king says: 'Go and strike this man with a hundred spears in the morning'. So, they struck the robber with a hundred spears in the morning. Then, at noon, the king asks: 'How is the robber?' 'Sire, he is still alive.' The king says: 'Go and strike the robber with another hundred spears at noon.' They struck the robber with another hundred spears at noon. Then, in the evening, the king asks: 'How is the robber?' 'Sire, he is still alive.' Then, the King says: 'Go and strike the robber with still another hundred spears in the evening.' They struck the robber with still another hundred spears in the evening."

"What do you think monks, because of being struck with the three hundred spears, would that man feel pain and grief?"

"Bhante, because of being struck with even one spear, that man would feel unbearable pain and grief, let alone three hundred spears."

Then, the Blessed One took a small stone in his grasp and addressed the monks thus: "What do you think monks? Which is greater, this small stone that I have taken in my grasp, or the Himalayas, king of mountains?"

"Bhante, the small stone that the Blessed One has taken in his grasp is nothing in comparison to the greatness of the Himalaya, the King of mountains. It is not even a fraction; it is beyond comparison."

"Similarly, monks, the pain and grief that a man would feel due to being struck by the three hundred spears is nothing in comparison to the suffering in Hell. It is not even a fraction; it is beyond comparison."

"Now, the wardens of hell torture him with the fivefold transfixing. They drive a red hot iron spike through one hand, they drive a red hot iron spike through the other hand, they drive a red hot iron spike through one foot, they drive a red hot iron spike through the other foot, and they drive a red hot iron spike through his chest. There, he feels painful, racking, piercing feelings. Yet, he does not die as long as his evil actions have not exhausted their result."

"Next, the wardens of hell throw him down and peel him with axes. There, he feels painful, racking, piercing feelings. Yet, he does not die as long as his evil actions have not exhausted their result."

"Next, the wardens of hell set him with his feet up and his head down and trim him with adzes. There, he feels painful, racking, piercing feelings. Yet, he does not die as long as his evil actions have not exhausted their result."

"Next, the wardens of hell tie him to a chariot and drive him back and forth on a floor that is burning, blazing, and glowing. There, he feels painful, racking, piercing feelings. Yet, he does not die as long as his evil actions have not exhausted their result."

"Next, the wardens of hell make him climb up and down a mountain of coals that are burning, blazing, and glowing. There, he feels painful, racking, piercing feelings. Yet, he does not die as long as his evil actions have not exhausted their result."

"Next, the wardens of hell take him feet up and head down plunge him into a red hot metal pot that is burning, blazing, and glowing, where he is cooked in the froth. He, now, floats up, down, and across. There, he feels painful, racking, piercing feelings. Yet, he does not die as long as his evil actions have not exhausted their result."

"Next, the wardens of hell throw him into the Great Hell. Monks, that great hell can be described thus:

It has four corners and is built with four doors, one set in each side.

It is covered all around with iron walls. It is shut with an iron roof.

Its floor, as well, is made of iron, and heated until it glows with fire.

The range is a full hundred leagues that spreads continuously."

"Monks, I could describe to you about Hell in many ways, but, still it is hard to finish describing the suffering in Hell."

(THE ANIMAL REALM)

"Monks, there are many animals that feed on grass. They eat fresh or dried grass by breaking it with their teeth. Monks, what animals feed on grass? Horses, cattle, donkeys, goats, deer, and any other such animals. Monks, a foolish human being having committed evil actions, in the pursuit of sensual pleasures, at the break-up of the body, after death, is reborn among the company of animals that feed on grass."

"Monks, there are animals that feed on dung. They smell dung from a distance and run to it thinking: 'We can eat here, we can eat here!' Just as Brāhmins run to the smell of food: 'We can eat here, we can eat here!', so too, monks, these animals that feed on dung, smell dung from a distance and run to it thinking: 'We can eat here, we can eat here!' Monks, what animals feed on dung? Chickens, pigs, dogs, jackals, and any other such animals. Monks, a foolish human being having committed evil actions, in the pursuit of sensual pleasures, at the break-up of the body, after death, is reborn among the company of animals that feed on dung."

"Monks, there are animals that are born in darkness, age in darkness, and die in darkness. Monks, what types of animals are born in darkness, age in darkness, and die in darkness? Moths, maggots, earthworms, and any other such animals. Monks, a foolish human being having committed evil actions, in the pursuit of sensual pleasures, at the break-up of the body, after death, is reborn among the company of animals that are born in darkness, age in darkness, and die in darkness."

"Monks, there are animals that are born in water, age in water, and die in water. Monks, what types of animals are born in water, age in water, and die in water? Fish, turtles, crocodiles, and any other such animals. Monks, a foolish human being having committed evil actions, in the pursuit of sensual pleasures, at the break-up of the body, after death, is reborn among the company of animals that are born in water, age in water, and die in water."

"Monks, there are animals that are born in filth, age in filth, and die in filth. Monks, what types of animals are born in filth, age in filth, and die in filth? Monks, the animals that are born in rotten fish, age in rotten fish, and die in rotten fish fall into this category. The animals that are born in a rotten corpse... or rotten porridge... or in a cesspit... or in a sewer... fall into this category. Monks, a foolish human being having committed evil actions, in the pursuit of sensual pleasures, at the break-up of the body, after death, is reborn among the company of animals that are born in filth, age in filth, and die in filth."

"Monks, I could describe to you about the animal realm in many ways, but, still it is hard to finish describing the suffering in the animal realm."

"Monks, suppose a man threw a piece of round wood with one hole in it into the ocean. The wind coming from the east carried it to the west, the wind coming from the west carried it to the east, the wind coming from the north carried it to the south, and the wind coming from the south carried it to the north. Suppose there was a blind turtle that came to the surface once every hundred years. What do you think monks? Would that blind turtle put his neck into the hole of the round wood?"

"He might Bhante, but, it would be after a long period of time."

"Monks, the blind turtle may put his neck into the hole of the round wood, sooner than a fool who once was born in a plane of misery would regain a birth in the human state, I say. Why is that? Because there is no practicing of the Dhamma there, no practicing of what is righteous, no doing of what is wholesome, and no collecting of merit. What is there is only the habit of devouring each other and the slaughter of the weak."

"Monks, at the end of a long period, one day, if that fool returns to the human state, he will be born into a low family — a family of outcasts, a family of hunters, a family of bamboo workers, a family of cart makers, or to a family of excrement carriers. There, he is extremely poor with little to eat and drink, surviving with much difficulty, and hardly finds food and clothing. He is ugly, unsightly, deformed, sickly, blind, with misshapen hands and legs, a dwarf, or paralyzed. He receives no food, drinks, clothes, vehicles, garlands, perfumes and cosmetics, bed, lodging, and light. He, again, misconducts in body, misconducts in speech, and misconducts in mind. Having misconducted in body, speech, and mind, at the break-up of the body, after death, he is reborn in the plane of misery - the worst destination: in Hell."

"Monks, suppose a gambler at the very first unlucky throw loses his child and his wife and all his wealth and eventually becomes nothing and is destined to prison. Yet, such an unlucky throw is nothing. What the biggest lost is that when a fool having misconducted in body, misconducted in speech, and misconducted in mind, at the break-up of the body, after death, has to be born in the plane of misery - the worst destination: in Hell. Monks, Hell is what is called the perfect destination for a fool."

(Abstracted from *Bālapaṇḍita Sutta*)

1.2 Devadūta Suttaṁ—The Divine Messengers

This is how I heard: One day, the Blessed One was living in the province of Sāvatthi, at Jeta's park in Anāthapiṇḍika's monastery. There, the Blessed One addressed the monks, saying "Monks." "Bhante" those monks replied. Then, the Blessed One taught the following discourse:

"Monks, imagine there were two houses with doors. There is a man with good eyesight standing in between them, watching. This man saw people entering and exiting these houses and staying and wandering inside. In the same way, monks, with the divine eye, which is purified and surpasses the human eye, I see beings passing away and beings born, inferior and superior, beautiful and ugly, fortunate and unfortunate. I see and understand those beings pass away and reborn according to their actions."

"These worthy beings, who were well conducted in body, speech, and mind did not insult the noble ones, had right view, and acted according to right view, after death, at the breaking up of the body, such beings were reborn in good destinations, possibly the heavenly worlds. Or these worthy beings, who were well conducted in body, speech, and mind, did not insult the noble ones, had right view, and acted according to right view, after death, at the breakup of the body, such beings were reborn in the human world."

"But, other beings who were ill conducted in body, speech, and mind, insulted the noble ones, had wrong view, and acted according to wrong view, after death, at the break-up of the body, such beings were born in the ghostly world, animal world, or in the worst destination, in hell." "Then, the hell wardens grab such a being by the arms and show him to King Yama, saying: 'Sire, this being, ill-treated his mother, father, recluses, and brāhmins; and he did not respect his family elders. Let the king decide his punishment."

"Now, King Yama interrogates, quizzes, and questions him about the first divine messenger. 'Hey being, didn't you see the first divine messenger among humans?' He replies: 'Venerable Sir, I did not.' Next, King Yama asks: 'Hey being, didn't you see among humans, a young baby lying smeared with his own urine and excrement?' He replies: 'Venerable Sir, I did."

"King Yama questions: 'Didn't it ever occur to you that as an intelligent, young man, that I, too, am subject to birth,

I, too, am not free from birth, therefore, I must do good by body, speech and mind?' He answers: 'I was very negligent; I was not able to do so, Venerable Sir.' King Yama says: 'Now, surely according to your negligence you have not done good by body, speech and mind. But, these evil actions weren't done by your mother, father, brother, sister, your friends, kinsmen, relatives, recluses, brāmins, or by gods. These evil actions were done by you alone, therefore, you must experience their result."

"After, interrogating, quizzing, and questioning him about the first divine messenger, King Yama interrogates, quizzes, and questions him about the second divine messenger. 'Hey being, didn't you see the second divine messenger among humans?' He says: 'Venerable Sir, I did not.' King Yama asks: 'Did you not ever see an old man or woman in the age of about eighty, ninety, or a hundred, very old, fragile, walking with a stick, shivering, hunched over, with a crooked back, grey haired, and with few teeth?' He replies: 'Venerable Sir, yes I did."

"King Yama questions: 'Didn't it ever occur to you that as an intelligent, young man, that I, too, am subject to old age, I, too, am not free from old age, therefore, I must do good by body, speech and mind?' He answers: 'I was very negligent; I was not able to do so Venerable Sir.' King Yama says: 'Now, surely according to your negligence you have not done good by body, speech and mind. But, these evil actions weren't done by your mother, father, brother, sister, your friends, kinsmen, relatives, recluses, brāmins, or by gods. These evil actions were done by you alone, therefore, you must experience their result."

"After interrogating, quizzing, and questioning him about the second divine messenger, King Yama interrogates, quizzes, and questions about the third divine messenger: 'Hey being, didn't you see the third divine messenger among humans?' He replies: 'Venerable Sir, I did not.' King Yama says: 'Hey being, didn't you ever see among humans, a man or a woman, very ill and sick, laying in their own urine and excrement, and who needs to be sat down by others and lifted up by others?' He replies: 'Venerable Sir, I did.'"

"King Yama questions: 'Didn't it ever occur to you that as an intelligent, young man, that I, too, am subject to illness, I, too, am not free from illness, therefore, I must do good by body, speech, and mind?' He answers: 'I was very negligent; I was not able to do so Venerable Sir.' King Yama says: 'Now, surely according to your negligence you have not done good by body, speech, and mind. But, these evil actions weren't done by your mother, father, brother, sister, your friends, kinsmen, relatives, recluses, brāmins, or by gods. These evil actions were done by you alone, therefore, you must experience their result.'"

"After interrogating, quizzing, and questioning him about the third divine messenger, King Yama interrogates, quizzes, questions about the fourth divine messenger. 'Hey being, didn't you see the fourth divine messenger among humans?' He answers: 'Venerable Sir, I did not.' King Yama says: 'Didn't you ever see among humans a robber or a burglar, captured and then punished in various ways: having him beaten with whips, beaten with canes, beaten with clubs, having his hands cut off, his feet cut of, his hands and feet cut off, his ears cut off, his nose cut off, his ears and nose cut off, having his head smashed, having his head shaved with gravel until the skull is visible, having his mouth opened with an iron hook and setting a fire torch in it, having his body wrapped with oily clothes then setting fire on the clothes, having his arms wrapped with oily clothes then setting fire on the clothes, having his skin removed from his neck to the bottom and dragged, having his skin removed from his neck downwards and from his feet upwards and tied them together, having put spikes through two knees and two elbows to the ground and gets burnt, having his body stabbed with hooks and smashed flesh, having his entire flesh torn into small pieces, having his entire body poked with holes and putting boiling oil into them, having him on his side and drilled a spike through his ears to the ground, then by holding his legs they spin him on the spot, having his bones broken into small pieces with stones, having him splashed with boiling oil, having him thrown to be devoured by dogs, being alive he is speared with spikes, and having his head cut off with a sword?"

"He answers: 'Venerable Sir, I did.' King Yama questions: 'Didn't it ever occur to you that as an intelligent, young man, when an evil-doer is caught and is punished with these various tortures here in this very life? Not to speak of punishments in the next life. Therefore, I must do good by body, speech, and mind?' He answers: 'I was very negligent; I was not able to do so Venerable Sir.' King Yama says: 'Now, surely according to your negligence you have not done good by body, speech, and mind. But, these evil actions weren't done by your mother, father, brother, sister, your friends, kinsmen, relatives, recluses, brāmins, or by gods. These evil actions were done by you alone, therefore, you must experience their result."

"After interrogating, quizzing, and questioning him about the fourth divine messenger, King Yama interrogates, quizzes, and questions him about the fifth divine messenger: 'Hey being, didn't you see the fifth divine messenger among humans'. He answers: 'Venerable Sir, I did not.' King Yama says: 'Didn't you ever see a man or a woman, dead for one day, dead for two days and dead for three days, swollen, black, and with oozing pus?' He answers: 'Venerable Sir, I did.'"

"King Yama questions: 'Didn't it ever occur to you that as an intelligent, young man, that I am also subject to death, I haven't overcome death. Therefore, I must do good by body, speech, and mind?' He answers: 'I was very negligent; I was not able to do so Venerable Sir.' King Yama says: 'Now, surely according to your negligence you have not done good by body, speech, and mind. But, these evil actions weren't done by your mother, father, brother, sister, your friends, kinsmen, relatives, recluses, brāmins ,or by gods. These evil actions were done by you alone, therefore, you must experience their result.'"

"Then, after interrogating, quizzing, and questioning him about the fifth divine messenger, King Yama became silent."

"Now, the wardens of hell torture him with the fivefold transfixing. They drive a red-hot iron rod through one hand; they drive a red-hot iron rod through the other hand; they drive a red-hot iron rod through one foot; they drive a red-hot iron rod through the other foot; and they drive a red-hot iron rod through his chest. There, he feels painful, racking, piercing feelings. Yet, he doesn't die as long as his evil actions have not exhausted their result."

"Next, the wardens of hell throw him down and peel him with axes. There, he feels painful, racking, piercing feelings. Yet, he doesn't die as long as his evil actions haven't exhausted their result."

"Next, the wardens of hell set him with his feet up and his head down and trim him with adzes. There, he feels painful, racking, piercing feelings. Yet, he doesn't die as long as his evil actions haven't exhausted their result."

"Next, the wardens of hell tie him to a chariot and drive him back and forth on a floor that is burning, blazing, and glowing. There, he feels painful, racking, piercing feelings. Yet, he doesn't die as long as his evil actions haven't exhausted their result."

"Next, the wardens of hell make him climb up and down a mountain of coals that are burning, blazing, and glowing. There, he feels painful, racking, piercing feelings. Yet, he doesn't die as long as his evil actions haven't exhausted their result."

"Next, the wardens of hell take him feet up and head down, and plunge him into a red hot metal pot that is burning, blazing, and glowing. He is cooked there in froth and he now floats up, down, and across. There, he feels painful, racking, piercing feelings. Yet, he doesn't die as long as his evil actions haven't exhausted their result."

"Next, the wardens of hell throw him into the Great Hell. Monks that great hell is as such:

It has four corners and is built with four doors, one set in each side.

It is covered all around with iron walls. It is shut with an iron roof.

Its floor, as well, is made of iron, and heated until it glows with fire.

The range is a full hundred leagues (700 km) that spreads continuously."

"Now, the flames that come out of the eastern wall dash against the western wall. The flames that come out of the western wall dash against the eastern wall. Then, the flames that come out of the northern wall dash against the southern wall, and the flames that come out of the southern wall dash against the northern wall. Also, the flames that come out of the top dash against the bottom and the flames that come out of the bottom dash against the top. There, he feels painful, racking, piercing feelings. Yet, he does not die as long as his evil actions haven't exhausted their result."

"At the end of a long period, monks, there comes a time when the Great Hell's eastern door is opened. He runs towards it quickly, and as he runs his outer skin burns, his inner skin burns, his flesh burns, his sinews burn, and his bones turn to smoke. It is the same when his foot is uplifted. After such long running, eventually, he reaches the door, then it is shut. There, he feels painful, racking, piercing feelings. Yet, he doesn't die as long as his evil actions haven't exhausted their result."

"At the end of a long period, monks, there comes a time when the Great Hell's western door is opened. He runs towards it quickly, and as he runs, his outer skin burns, his inner skin burns, his flesh burns, his sinews burn, and his bones turn to smoke. It is the same when his foot is lifted up. After such long running, eventually, he reaches the door, then it is shut. There, he feels painful, racking, piercing feelings. Yet, he doesn't die as long as his evil actions haven't exhausted their result."

"At the end of a long period, monks, there comes a time when the Great Hell's northern door is opened. He runs towards it quickly, and as he runs, his outer skin burns, his inner skin burns, his flesh burns, his sinews burn, and his bones turn to smoke. It is the same when his foot is lifted up. After such long running, eventually, he reaches the door, then it is shut. There, he feels painful, racking, piercing feelings. Yet, he doesn't die as long as his evil actions haven't exhausted their result."

"At the end of a long period, monks, there comes a time when the Great Hell's southern door is opened. He runs towards it quickly, and as he runs, his outer skin burns, his inner skin burns, his flesh burns, his sinews burn, and his bones turn to smoke. It is the same when his foot is lifted up. After such long running, eventually, he reaches the door, then it is shut. There, he feels painful, racking, piercing feelings. Yet, he doesn't die as long as his evil actions haven't exhausted their results."

"At the end of a long period, monks, there comes a time when the Great Hell's eastern door is reopened. He runs towards it quickly, and as he runs, his outer skin burns, his inner skin burns, his flesh burns, his sinews burn, and his bones turn to smoke. It is the same when his foot is lifted up. But he comes out from that door."

"Immediately next to the Great Hell is the vast Hell of Excrement. He falls into the Hell of Excrement. There, needle mouthed creatures pierce through his outer skin. Having pierced through his outer skin, they pierce through his inner skin. Having pierced through his inner skin, they pierce through his flesh. Having pierced through his flesh, they pierce through his sinews. Having pierced through his sinews, they pierce through his bones. Having pierced through his bones, they devour his bone marrow. There, he feels painful, racking, piercing feelings. Yet, he doesn't die as long as his evil actions haven't exhausted their result."

"Immediately next to the Hell of Excrement is the vast Hell of Hot Embers. He falls into the Hell of Hot Embers. There, he feels painful, racking, piercing feelings. Yet, he doesn't die as long as his evil actions haven't exhausted their result."

"Immediately next to the Hell of Hot Embers is the vast Wood of Simbali Trees, a league high (7 km), rising with thorns sixteen finger-breadths long, burning, blazing and glowing. They make him climb up and down those trees. There, he feels painful, racking, piercing feelings. Yet, he doesn't die as long as his evil actions haven't exhausted their result."

"Immediately next to the Wood of Simbali Trees is the vast Wood of Sword-leaf Trees. He runs there. The leaves, stirred up by the wind, cut his hands, cut his feet, cut his hands and feet, cut his ears, cut his nose, and cut his ears and nose. There, he feels painful, racking, piercing feelings. Yet, he doesn't die as long as his evil actions haven't exhausted their result."

"Immediately next to the Wood of Sword-Leaf Trees is the Great River of Acid Water. He falls into that. There, he is swept along the stream and against the stream and both along and against the stream. There, he feels painful, racking, piercing feelings. Yet, he doesn't die as long as his evil actions haven't exhausted their result."

"Next, the wardens of hell pull him out with a hook, and throw him on the ground. They ask him: 'Hey being, what do you want?' He says: 'Venerable Sirs, I am very hungry.' Then the wardens of hell open his mouth with extremely heated red-hot iron tongs, burning, blazing and glowing, and they throw into his mouth a red-hot metal ball, burning, blazing, and glowing. It burns his lips; it burns his mouth; it burns his throat; and it burns his stomach. It passes into his intestines and mesentery. There, he feels painful, racking, piercing feelings. Yet, he doesn't die as long as his evil actions haven't exhausted their result."

"Next, the wardens of hell pull him out with a hook, and throw him on the ground. They ask him: 'Hey being, what do you want?' He says: 'Venerable Sirs, I am very thirsty.' Then the wardens of hell open his mouth with extremely heated red- hot iron tongs, burning, blazing and glowing, and they pour into his mouth molten copper, burning, blazing, and glowing. It burns his lips; it burns his mouth; it burns his throat; and it burns his stomach. It passes into his intestines and mesentery. There, he feels painful, racking, piercing feelings. Yet, he doesn't die as long as his evil actions haven't exhausted their result."

"Then, the wardens of hell throw him back again into the Great Hell."

"One day, monks, it occurred to King Yama: 'In this world, beings that do evil, unwholesome actions, indeed are punished with many types of tortures. Oh, I wish that I may gain the human life and a Tathāgata, fully enlightened

Buddha, may appear in the world, and I may go to the Blessed One to listen to the Dhamma, and the Blessed One may teach me the Dhamma, and I may understand the Blessed One's Dhamma!"

"Monks, I tell you this not as something I heard from another recluse or brāmin. I tell you this as something that I have actually known, seen, and realized by myself."

This discourse was taught by the Blessed One. Having taught this, the Sublime One, the Great Teacher further said:

"Even when warned by the divine messengers, some people still do bad things. They will go to the lower world, hell, and they will experience sorrow there for a long time. When, in this world, good people are warned by the divine messengers, they do not do bad things, but practice the noble Dhamma well. Having seen the fear of clinging which produces rebirth and death, they are freed by not clinging and destroying birth and death. They, here and now, reach Nibbāna - safety from all fears, supreme peace. Having overcome all fear and hatred, they have escaped from all suffering in Saṁsāra."

1.3 Kokālika Suttaṁ—Discourse about Kokālika

At Sāvatthi, one day, the monk Kokālika went to the Blessed One. Having paid homage to the Blessed One, he sat down to one side, and said "Bhante, Arahants Sāriputta and Moggallāna have evil wishes; they are intoxicated with evil wishes."

When this was said, the Blessed One said to the monk Kokālika "Do not speak in that way, Kokālika! Place confidence in Sāriputta and Moggallāna, Kokālika. Sāriputta and Moggallāna are well behaved."

A second time the monk Kokālika said to the Blessed One "Bhante, although I have confidence and trust in the Blessed One, still I say Arahants Sāriputta and Moggallāna have evil wishes; they are intoxicated with evil wishes."

A second time the Blessed One said to the monk Kokālika "Do not speak in that way, Kokālika! Place confidence in Sāriputta and Moggallāna, Kokālika. Sāriputta and Moggallāna are well behaved."

A third time the monk Kokālika said to the Blessed One "Bhante, even though I have confidence and trust in the Blessed One, still I say Arahants Sāriputta and Moggallāna have evil wishes; they are intoxicated with evil wishes."

A third time the Blessed One said to the monk Kokālika "Do not speak in that way, Kokālika! Place confidence in Sāriputta and Moggallāna, Kokālika. Sāriputta and Moggallāna are well behaved."

Then, monk Kokālika arose from his seat, paid homage to the Blessed One, and departed worshiping around the Blessed One. Not long after the monk Kokālika had left, his entire body became covered with boils the size of mustard seeds. These then grew to the size of mung beans; then to the size of chickpeas; then to the size of jujube stones; then to the size of jujube fruits; then to the size of myrobalans; then to the size of unripe beluva fruits; and then to the size of ripe beluva fruits. When the boils had grown to the size of ripe beluva fruits, they burst open, oozing pus and blood. Then on account of that illness, the monk Kokālika died, and because he had rivalry towards Arahant Sāriputta and

Arahant Moggallāna, after his death he was reborn in the Paduma hell.

Then, when the night was ending, Brahma Sahampati, of stunning beauty, illuminating the entire Jeta's Grove, went to the Blessed One, paid homage to the Buddha, stood to one side and said to Him"Bhante, the monk Kokālika has died, and because he had rivalry towards Arahant Sāriputta and Arahant Moggallāna, after his death he has been reborn in the Paduma hell." Having said this, he paid homage to the Blessed One, and after worshiping around the Blessed One, he disappeared.

When the night had ended, the Blessed One told the monks "Monks, last night, when the night was ending, Brahma Sahampati came to me and said to me 'Bhante, the monk Kokālika has died, and because he had rivalry towards Arahant Sāriputta and Arahant Moggallāna, after his death he has been reborn in the Paduma hell.' Having said this, he paid homage to me, and after worshiping around me, he disappeared."

After this was said, a certain monk asked the Blessed One "Bhante, how long is the life span in the Paduma hell?"

"Monk, the life span in the Paduma hell is very long. It is not easy to count and say that it is so many years, so many hundreds of years, so many thousands of years, or so many hundreds of thousands of years."

"Bhante, is it possible to give a simile?"

"Monk, it is possible. Suppose, there was a Kosalan cartload filled with twenty measures of sesame seeds. At the end of every hundred years a man would remove one seed from there. That Kosalan cartload of twenty measures of sesame seeds, by this effort, would be used up and eliminated more quickly than the lifespan of a single Abbuda hell. The lifespan of twenty Abbuda hells is equal to one Nirabbuda hell lifespan; the lifespan of twenty Nirabbuda hells is equal to one Ababa hell lifespan; the lifespan of twenty Ababa hells is equal to one Atata hell lifespan; the lifespan of twenty Atata hells is equal to one Ahaha hell lifespan; the lifespan of twenty Ahaha hells is equal to one Kumuda hell lifespan; the lifespan of twenty Kumuda hells is equal to one Sogandhika hell lifespan; the lifespan of twenty Sogandhika hells is equal to one Uppala hell lifespan; the lifespan of twenty Uppala hells is equal to one Pundarika hell lifespan; and the lifespan of twenty Pundarika hells is equal to one Paduma hell lifespan. Monk, now the monk Kokālika has been reborn in the Paduma hell because he had hatred towards Arahant Sāriputta and Arahant Moggallāna."

This is what the Blessed One said. Having said this, the Well Gone One, the Great Teacher further said thus:

"When a fool takes birth, an axe is born inside his mouth, with which the fool cuts himself speaking harsh words."

"He who praises a person deserving criticism, or criticises a person deserving praise, collects a lot of demerit with his mouth. Because of that evil deed, he will never find happiness."

"Insignificant is the unlucky throw that brings the loss of all wealth including oneself at dice; worse by far, is this unlucky throw of giving rise to hatred toward liberated ones."

"The insulter of noble ones, having done evil with speech and mind goes to hell. There, he has to suffer for a hundred thousand Nirabbudas, and thirty six more, and five Abbudas."

"The one who charges another untruthfully goes to Hell. Again, the one having done evil says, 'I did not do it', also goes to Hell. In the next world, both become equal. Evildoers suffer in the next world."

"Whoever offends against someone who never hates, is pure and unblemished, the result of that evil kamma rebounds that fool, like fine dust thrown against the wind."

"The one who scolds others with harsh speech, is devoid of faith, stingy, lacks Dhamma knowledge, hoards his belongings, and speaks divisively is enslaved by greed."

"You, oh foul mouthed, outcast, evil, wicked, the lowest of men, lowest of birth, do not speak much here! Do not fall into Hell."

"You, oh evildoer, you scatter dust of defilements upon yourself and bring downfall upon you. You disparage noble people. Having done many evil things, you will fall into the depths of Hell and stay there for a long time."

"One's actions do not disappear without reaping its result. The doer of the action indeed is the owner of the result. The evildoer, the fool, sees misery for himself in the next world."

"He will be born in a Hell, which is set with iron spikes with sharp blades. There are blazing iron balls as food that appears according to kamma."

"The wardens of Hell never address Hell beings pleasantly. They do not care for him or take him to safety. Instead they spread embers and enter a fire blazing around them."

"They envelop the Hell being with an iron net and strike him with hammers made of iron."

"Next, he falls into a huge pot made of iron full of blazing fire. He's cooked in it for a long time, floating about in the masses of fire."

"Then, the evildoer is boiled in a mixture of pus and blood. Whichever direction he turns, he is attacked by pus and blood."

"The evildoer is cooked in water full of worms. There is not even a bank visible to escape. The cooking pot is made all around with an iron wall."

"Next, the Hell being enters a Hell called Forest of Sharp-Edged Sword Blades. In that Hell, his hands and legs are cut to pieces by these sharp leaves. Pulling his tongue with a hook, the wardens of Hell torture him repeatedly."

"Next, the Hell being approaches a Hell called Vetaraṇī, very hard to cross, with sharp edged blades and razors. Evil fools having done evil, fall into this Hell."

"While Hell beings are wailing there, black and spotted dogs, ravens, jackals, vultures, hawks, and crows devour them. Hell beings' bodies are torn apart by these creatures."

"Hard indeed is the life in hell where an evildoer experiences much pain. Therefore, in the remainder of his life, here in this human world, one should practice the Dhamma and perform wholesome acts diligently."

"When an evildoer is born in Paduma Hell, his lifespan there is calculated by the wise and compared to the loads of sesame seeds. They are five crores of nahuta and again twelve hundred crores in addition."

"Various types of suffering in miserable Hells have been described here. Hell beings must stay there for a long time suffering immensely. Therefore, one should always protect one's speech and thoughts toward those who are pure, virtuous, and have noble qualities."

1.4 Niraya Sutta—Causes to be Reborn in Hell

This is as I heard: One day, the Blessed One was living in the city of Sāvatthi, at Jeta's park in Anāthapindika's monastery. The Blessed One addressed the monks saying "Monks." "Bhante" they replied. Then, the Blessed One taught this discourse:

"Monks, the person with these ten qualities will be reborn in hell as quickly as if a heavy load was suddenly lowered from one's head. What are these ten qualities?"

(1) "Monks, in this world, someone kills beings; he is murderous, bloody handed, uses weapons and engages in violence, and is cruel to living beings."

(2) "He steals the wealth and property of others in the village or forest."

(3) "He commits sexual misconduct. He has sexual relations with women who are protected by their mother, father, mother and father, brother, sister, or relatives; who are protected by noble qualities; who have a husband; or even with one already engaged."

(4) "He lies if he is summoned to a council, to an assembly, to his relatives' presence, or to the court, and questioned as a witness thus: 'So, speak of what you know,' then, not knowing, he says, 'I know,' or knowing, he says, 'I do not know'; not seeing, he says, 'I see,' or seeing, he says, 'I do not see.' In this way, he deliberately lies for his own sake, another's sake, or for some worldly gain."

(5) "He speaks divisively. Having heard something here, he repeats it elsewhere in order to divide one group from another; or having heard something elsewhere, he repeats it to the other group in order to divide the two groups. In this way, he is one who divides those who are united, a destroyer of friendships, one who enjoys division, rejoices in division, delights in divisions, and a speaker of words that create division."

(6) "He speaks harshly. He speaks words that are rough, hard, hurtful to others, offensive to others, that give rise to anger, and words that destroy peace of others."

(7) "He speaks idly. He speaks at an improper time, speaks falsely, speaks of what is meaningless, speaks against the natural law of the world, speaks of what leads to bad behavior, speaks at an improper time, and speaks words that are worthless of memorizing, unreasonable, rambling, and unbeneficial."

(8) "He is full of desires. He craves for the wealth and property of others thus: 'Oh, what belongs to others be mine!'"

(9) "He has a mind of ill will and intentions of hate thus: 'May these beings be slain, slaughtered, cut off, destroyed, or fall into calamity."

(10) "He holds wrong views and has misleading ideas thus: 'There is no result of giving and sharing, there is no result of offerings, there is no result of helping others, there is no result of good or bad actions, there is no such world called this world, there is no such world called next world, one's mother is not a special person to them, one's father is not a special person to them, there are no beings spontaneously reborn (hell beings, ghostly beings, heavenly beings), and in this world, there are no superior people of right conduct and practice, who, having realized of the true nature of this world and the other world for themselves by direct knowledge, disclose the reality of the world to others."

"Monks, the person with these ten qualities will be reborn in hell as quickly as if a heavy load was suddenly lowered from one's head."

(From Niraya Suttaṁ)

1.5 Apāyasaṁvattanika Suttaṁ—Actions that Lead to Rebirth in the Planes of Misery

This is as I heard: One day, the Blessed One was living in the city of Sāvatthi, at Jeta's park in Anāthapindika's monastery. The Blessed One addressed the monks saying "Monks." "Bhante" they replied. Then, the Blessed One taught this discourse:

(1) "Monks, when one kills beings constantly and repeatedly, one is subject to be reborn in hell, the animal world, or in the ghost world. Whenever this person is reborn as

a human being, the remaining result of killing beings ripens and causes a shorter life span."

(2) "Monks, when one steals constantly and repeatedly, one is subject to be reborn in hell, the animal world, or in the ghost world. Whenever this person is reborn as a human being, the remaining result of stealing ripens and causes the loss of his wealth."

(3) "Monks, when one commits sexual misconduct constantly and repeatedly, one is subject to be reborn in hell, the animal world, or in the ghost world. Whenever this person is reborn as a human being, the remaining result of sexual misconduct ripens and causes the attacks of revenge by his enemies."

(4) "Monks, when one lies constantly and repeatedly, one is subject to be reborn in hell, the animal world, or in the ghost world. Whenever this person is reborn as a human being, the remaining result of lying ripens and causes false accusations."

(5) "Monks, when one speaks divisively constantly and repeatedly, one is subject to be reborn in hell, the animal world, or in the ghost world. Whenever this person is reborn as a human being, the remaining result of divisive speech ripens and causes the division from his friends."

(6) "Monks, when one speaks harshly constantly and repeatedly, one is subject to be reborn in hell, the animal world, or in the ghost world. Whenever this person is reborn as a human being, the remaining result of harsh speech ripens and causes disliked sounds."

(7) "Monks, when one speaks idly constantly and repeatedly,

one is subject to be reborn in hell, the animal world, or in the ghost world. Whenever this person is reborn as a human being, the remaining result of idle chatter ripens and causes distrust on whatever he says."

(8) "Monks, when one takes intoxicating drinks and drugs constantly and repeatedly, one is subject to be reborn in hell, the animal world, or in the ghost world. Whenever this person is reborn as a human being, the remaining result of taking intoxicating drinks and drugs ripens and causes an incurable mental illness."

1.6 Saṁsappanīya Pariyāya Suttaṁ —Animals that Curl Up

"Monks, I will teach you the Dhamma on the destiny of animals that curl up. Listen and understand well. I will speak." "Yes, Bhante," those monks replied. The Blessed One taught the following discourse:

"Monks, what is the meaning of the Dhamma on the destiny of animals that curl up? Monks, beings are the owners of their kamma and the heirs of their kamma. Kamma decides their rebirth, kamma is their relative, kamma is their refuge, and whatever kamma they do, good or bad, they deserve its result."

(1) "Monks, in this world, someone kills beings; he is murderous, bloody handed, uses weapons and engages in violence, and is cruel to living beings. He curls up his body, speech, and mind. His bodily kamma is not straight but deceitful, his verbal kamma is not straight

but deceitful, and his mental kamma is not straight but deceitful. As a result, his destination is not straight but curling. His rebirth is not straight but curling. Monks, for one with a curling destination and rebirth, I say, there are two possible places of rebirth, either the exclusively painful hell or among species of animals that curl up. Monks, what are the species of curling animals? Snakes, scorpions, centipedes, mongooses, cats, mice, owls, and any other animals that curl up when they see people. Therefore, monks, a being's action determines his rebirth. One is reborn through one's deeds. When one has been reborn, one experiences the results of one's action. Monks, it is in this way, I say, that beings are the heirs of their Kamma."

(2)   "Monks, in this world someone steals the wealth and property of others in the village or forest. He curls up his body, speech, and mind. His bodily kamma is not straight but deceitful, his verbal kamma is not straight but deceitful, and his mental kamma is not straight but deceitful. As a result, his destination is not straight but curling. His rebirth is not straight but curling. Monks, for one with a curling destination and rebirth, I say, there are two possible places of rebirth, either the exclusively painful hell or among species of animals that curl up. Monks, what are the species of curling animals? Snakes, scorpions, centipedes, mongooses, cats, mice, owls, and any other animals that curl up when they see people. Therefore monks, a being's action determines his rebirth. One is reborn through one's deeds. When one has been reborn, one experiences the results of one's action. Monks, it is in this way, I say, that beings are the heirs of their Kamma."

(3) "Monks, in this world someone commits sexual misconduct. He has sexual relations with women who are protected by their mother, father, mother and father, brother, sister, or relatives; who are protected by noble qualities; who have a husband; or even with one already engaged. He curls along by body, speech, and mind. His bodily kamma is not straight but curling; his verbal kamma is not straight but curling; and his mental kamma is not straight but curling. His destination is not straight but curling and his rebirth is not straight but curling. Monks, for one with a curling destination and rebirth, I say, there are two possible places of rebirth: either the exclusively painful hell or among species of curling animals. Monks, what are the species of curling animals? Snakes, scorpions, centipedes, mongooses, cats, mice, and owls, or any other animals that curl when they see people. Therefore, monks, a being's action determines his rebirth; one is reborn through one's deeds;and when one has been reborn one experiences the results of one's action. Monks, it is in this way, I say, that beings are the heirs of their Kamma."

(4) "Monks, in this world someone lies if he is summoned to a council, to an assembly, to his relatives' presence, or to the court, and questioned as a witness thus: 'So, speak of what you know,' then, not knowing, he says, 'I know,' or knowing, he says, 'I do not know'; not seeing, he says, 'I see,' or seeing, he says, 'I do not see.' In this way, he deliberately lies for his own sake, another's sake, or for some worldly gain. He curls up his body, speech, and mind. His bodily kamma is not straight but deceitful, his verbal kamma is not straight but deceitful,

and his mental kamma is not straight but deceitful. As a result, his destination is not straight but curling. His rebirth is not straight but curling. Monks, for one with a curling destination and rebirth, I say, there are two possible places of rebirth, either the exclusively painful hell or among species of animals that curl up. Monks, what are the species of curling animals? Snakes, scorpions, centipedes, mongooses, cats, mice, owls, and any other animals that curl up when they see people. Therefore, monks, a being's action determines his rebirth. One is reborn through one's deeds. When one has been reborn, one experiences the results of one's action. Monks, it is in this way, I say, that beings are the heirs of their Kamma."

(5) "Monks, in this world someone speaks divisively. Having heard something here, he repeats it elsewhere in order to divide one group from another; or having heard something elsewhere, he repeats it to the other group in order to divide the two groups. In this way, he is one who divides those who are united, a destroyer of friendships, one who enjoys division, rejoices in division, delights in divisions, and a speaker of words that create division. He curls up his body, speech, and mind. His bodily kamma is not straight but deceitful, his verbal kamma is not straight but deceitful, and his mental kamma is not straight but deceitful. As a result, his destination is not straight but curling. His rebirth is not straight but curling. Monks, for one with a curling destination and rebirth, I say, there are two possible places of rebirth, either the exclusively painful hell or among species of animals that curl up. Monks, what are the species of curling animals? Snakes, scorpions,

centipedes, mongooses, cats, mice, owls, and any other
animals that curl up when they see people. Therefore,
monks, a being's action determines his rebirth. One
is reborn through one's deeds. When one has been
reborn, one experiences the results of one's action.
Monks, it is in this way, I say, that beings are the heirs
of their Kamma."

(6) "Monks, in this world someone speaks harshly. He
speaks words that are rough, hard, hurtful to others,
offensive to others, that give rise to anger, and words
that destroy peace of others. He curls up his body,
speech, and mind. His bodily kamma is not straight but
deceitful, his verbal kamma is not straight but deceitful,
and his mental kamma is not straight but deceitful.
As a result, his destination is not straight but curling.
His rebirth is not straight but curling. Monks, for one
with a curling destination and rebirth, I say, there are
two possible places of rebirth, either the exclusively
painful hell or among species of animals that curl
up. Monks, what are the species of curling animals?
Snakes, scorpions, centipedes, mongooses, cats, mice,
owls, and any other animals that curl up when they see
people. Therefore, monks, a being's action determines
his rebirth. One is reborn through one's deeds. When
one has been reborn, one experiences the results of
one's action. Monks, it is in this way, I say, that beings
are the heirs of their Kamma."

(7) "Monks, in this world someone speaks idly. He speaks
at an improper time, speaks falsely, speaks what is
meaningless, speaks against the natural law of the
world, speaks of what leads to bad behavior, speaks

at an improper time, and he speaks words that are not worthy of memorizing, unreasonable, rambling, and unbeneficial. He curls up his body, speech, and mind. His bodily kamma is not straight but deceitful, his verbal kamma is not straight but deceitful, and his mental kamma is not straight but deceitful. As a result, his destination is not straight but curling. His rebirth is not straight but curling. Monks, for one with a curling destination and rebirth, I say, there are two possible places of rebirth, either the exclusively painful hell or among species of animals that curl up. Monks, what are the species of curling animals? Snakes, scorpions, centipedes, mongooses, cats, mice, owls, and any other animals that curl up when they see people. Therefore, monks, a being's action determines his rebirth. One is reborn through one's deeds. When one has been reborn, one experiences the results of one's action. Monks, it is in this way, I say, that beings are the heirs of their Kamma."

(8) "Monks, in this world someone is full of desires. He craves for the wealth and property of others thus: 'Oh, what belongs to others be mine!' He curls up his body, speech, and mind. His bodily kamma is not straight but deceitful, his verbal kamma is not straight but deceitful, and his mental kamma is not straight but deceitful. As a result, his destination is not straight but curling. His rebirth is not straight but curling. Monks, for one with a curling destination and rebirth, I say, there are two possible places of rebirth, either the exclusively painful hell or among species of animals that curl up. Monks, what are the species of curling animals? Snakes, scorpions, centipedes, mongooses, cats, mice,

owls, and any other animals that curl up when they see people. Therefore, monks, a being's action determines his rebirth. One is reborn through one's deeds. When one has been reborn, one experiences the results of one's action. Monks, it is in this way, I say, that beings are the heirs of their Kamma."

(9) "Monks, in this world someone has a mind of ill will and intentions of hate thus: 'May these beings be slain, slaughtered, cut off, destroyed, or fall into calamity.' He curls up his body, speech, and mind. His bodily kamma is not straight but deceitful, his verbal kamma is not straight but deceitful, and his mental kamma is not straight but deceitful. As a result, his destination is not straight but curling. His rebirth is not straight but curling. Monks, for one with a curling destination and rebirth, I say, there are two possible places of rebirth, either the exclusively painful hell or among species of animals that curl up. Monks, what are the species of curling animals? Snakes, scorpions, centipedes, mongooses, cats, mice, owls, and any other animals that curl up when they see people. Therefore, monks, a being's action determines his rebirth. One is reborn through one's deeds. When one has been reborn, one experiences the results of one's action. Monks, it is in this way, I say, that beings are the heirs of their Kamma."

(10) "Monks, in this world someone holds wrong views and has misleading ideas thus: 'There is no result of giving and sharing, there is no result of offerings, there is no result of helping others, there is no result of good or bad actions, there is no such world called

this world, there is no such world called next world, one's mother is not a special person to them, one's father is not a special person to them, there are no beings spontaneously reborn (hell beings, ghostly beings, heavenly beings), and in this world, there are no superior people of right conduct and practice, who, having realized of the true nature of this worlds and the other worlds for themselves by direct knowledge, disclose the reality of the world to others.' He curls up his body, speech, and mind. His bodily kamma is not straight but deceitful, his verbal kamma is not straight but deceitful, and his mental kamma is not straight but deceitful. As a result, his destination is not straight but curling. His rebirth is not straight but curling. Monks, for one with a curling destination and rebirth, I say, there are two possible places of rebirth, either the exclusively painful hell or among species of animals that curl up. Monks, what are the species of curling animals? Snakes, scorpions, centipedes, mongooses, cats, mice, owls, and any other animals that curl up when they see people. Therefore, monks, a being's action determines his rebirth. One is reborn through one's deeds. When one has been reborn, one experiences the results of one's action. Monks, it is in this way, I say, that beings are the heirs of their Kamma."

"Monks, beings are the owners of their kamma and the heirs of their kamma. Kamma decides their rebirth, kamma is their relative, kamma is their refuge, and whatever kamma they do, good or bad, they deserve its result."

(From Saṁsappanīya Pariyāya Suttaṁ)

1.7 Sankhadhama Suttaṁ—The Conch Blower

On one occasion, the Blessed One was staying in the city of Nālandā at the Pāvārika Mango Grove. One day, Asibandhakaputta (blacksmith) Gāmani, a disciple of the Niganthas (the founder of Jainism), went to the Buddha, and on arrival, having worshipped the Buddha, sat to one side. As he was sitting there, the Buddha asked Gamani: "Dear Gāmani, how does Nigaṇṭha Nātaputta teach the Dhamma to his disciples?"

Gamani replied: "Bhante, Nigaṇṭha Nātaputta teaches the Dhamma to his disciples in this way: 'All those who kill will be reborn in hell. All those who steal will be reborn in hell. All those who commit sexual misconduct will be reborn in hell. All those who tell lies will be reborn in hell. Whatever one does frequently, such actions take one to hell.' Bhante, that's how Nigaṇṭha Nātaputta teaches the Dhamma to his disciples."

"Dear Gāmani, if it's true that 'Whatever one does frequently, such actions take one to hell,' then no one will be reborn in Hell in line with Nigaṇṭha Nātaputta's words.

(1) What do you think, dear Gāmani: If a man kills beings, consider the time spent killing and not killing, whether by day or by night, which time is more: the time he spends killing or not killing?"

(1) "Bhante, if a man kills beings, then taking into consideration the time spent killing and not killing, whether by day or by night, then the time he spends killing is less, and the time he spends not killing is certainly more."

(1) "See, dear Gāmani, if it's true that 'Whatever one does frequently, such actions take one to hell,' then no one will be reborn in Hell in line with Nigaṇṭha Nātaputta's words.

(2) What do you think, dear Gāmani: If a man steals, consider the time spent stealing and not stealing, whether by day or by night, which time is more: the time he spends stealing or not stealing?"

(2) "Bhante, if a man steals, then taking into consideration the time spent stealing and not stealing, whether by day or by night, then the time he spends stealing is less, and the time he spends not stealing is certainly more."

(2) "See, dear Gāmani, if it's true that 'Whatever one does frequently, such actions take one to hell,' then no one will be reborn in Hell in line with Nigaṇṭha Nātaputta's words.

(3) What do you think, dear Gāmani: If a man commits sexual misconduct, consider the time spent committing sexual misconduct and not committing sexual misconduct, whether by day or by night, which time is more: the time he spends committing sexual misconduct or not committing sexual misconduct ?"

(3) "Bhante, if a man commits sexual misconduct, then taking into consideration the time spent committing sexual misconduct and not committing sexual misconduct, whether by day or by night, then the time he spends

committing sexual misconduct is less, and the time he spends not committing sexual misconduct is certainly more."

(3) "See, dear Gāmani, if it's true that 'Whatever one does frequently, such actions take one to hell,' then no one will be reborn in Hell in line with Nigaṇṭha Nātaputta's words.

(4) What do you think, dear Gāmani: If a man tells lies, consider the time spent lying and not lying, whether by day or by night, which time is more: the time he spends lying or not lying?"

(4) "Bhante, if a man tells lies, then taking into consideration the time spent lying and not lying, whether by day or by night, then the time he spends lying is less, and the time he spends not lying is certainly more."

(4) "See, dear Gāmani, if it's true that 'Whatever one does frequently, such actions take one to hell,' then no one will be reborn in Hell in line with Nigaṇṭha Nātaputta's words."

"Dear Gāmani, there's the case where a certain teacher holds this doctrine, holds this view: 'All those who kill beings are reborn in hell. All those who steal are reborn in hell. All those who commit sexual misconduct are reborn in hell. All those who tell lies are reborn in hell.'

Dear Gāmani, a disciple has faith in that teacher, and the following thoughts occurs to him :

(1) 'My teacher preaches thus, holds such a view: "All those who kill beings are reborn in hell." In this case, I have killed beings before. Then surely, I will be reborn in hell." ' He holds onto that view. If he doesn't abandon such words, such mentality, and such view, he will be reborn in hell. He falls into hell as if a heavy load was dropped instantly from somebody's head.

(2) 'My teacher preaches thus, holds such a view: "All those who steal are reborn in hell." In this case, I have stolen before. Then surely, I will be reborn in hell."' He holds onto that view. If he doesn't abandon such words, such mentality, and such view, he will be reborn in hell. He falls into hell as if a heavy load was dropped instantly from somebody's head.

(3) 'My teacher preaches thus, holds such a view: "All those who commit sexual misconduct are reborn in hell." In this case, I have committed sexual misconduct before. Then surely, I will be reborn in hell."' He holds onto that view. If he doesn't abandon such words, such mentality, and such view, he will be reborn in hell. He falls into hell as if a heavy load was dropped instantly from somebody's head.

(4) 'My teacher preaches thus, holds such a view: "All those who lie are reborn in hell." In this case, I have lied before. Then surely, I will be reborn in hell."' He holds onto that view. If he doesn't abandon such words, such mentality, and such view, he will be reborn in hell. He falls into hell as if a heavy load was dropped instantly from somebody's head."

"Dear Gāmani, there is the case, where the Buddha appears in the world, worthy and self-awakened, perfect in true knowledge and pure conduct, follower of the noble path, the knower of worlds, unsurpassed teacher of taming persons, teacher of gods and humans, awakened, the blessed one. He, in various ways, criticizes and censures the act of killing beings, and says, 'Abstain from killing beings.' He criticizes and censures stealing, and says, 'Abstain from stealing.' He criticizes and censures committing sexual misconduct, and says, 'Abstain from committing sexual misconduct.' He criticizes and censures lying, and says, 'Abstain from lying."

"Then, dear Gāmani, a disciple has faith in the Buddha and reflects wisely:

(1) 'The Buddha in a variety of ways criticizes and censures killing beings, and says, "Abstain from killing." Yet, there are living beings that I have killed, to a greater or lesser extent. That was not right. That was not good. But if I become regretful of my evil act, that evil deed of mine will not be undone.' So, reflecting thus wisely, he stops the act of killing beings, and makes the determination to not kill in the future. Such thinking pattern leads to the eradication of the previously done evil and transcends the previously accumulated bad karma.

(2) 'The Buddha in a variety of ways criticizes and censures stealing, and says, "Abstain from stealing." Yet, there are things that I have stolen, to a greater or lesser extent. That was not right. That was not good. But if I become regretful of my evil act, that evil deed of mine will not be undone.' So, reflecting thus wisely, he stops the act of stealing, and makes the determination

to not steal in the future. Such thinking pattern leads to the eradication of the previously done evil and transcends the previously accumulated bad karma.

(3) 'The Buddha in a variety of ways criticizes and censures committing sexual misconduct, and says, "Abstain from sexual misconduct." Yet, there are times that I have committed sexual misconduct, to a greater or lesser extent. That was not right. That was not good. But if I become regretful of my evil act, that evil deed of mine will not be undone.' So, reflecting thus wisely, he stops the act of committing sexual misconduct, and makes the determination to not commit sexual misconduct in the future. Such thinking pattern leads to the eradication of the previously done evil and transcends the previously accumulated bad karma.

(4) 'The Buddha in a variety of ways criticizes and censures lying, and says, "Abstain from lying." Yet, there are times that I have lied, to a greater or lesser extent. That was not right. That was not good. But if I become regretful of my evil act, that evil deed of mine will not be undone.' So, reflecting thus wisely, he stops the act of lying, and makes the determination to not lie in the future. Such thinking pattern leads to the eradication of the previously done evil and transcends the previously accumulated bad karma."

"Having abandoned killing beings, he refrains from killing beings. Having abandoned stealing, he refrains from stealing. Having abandoned sexual misconduct, he refrains from sexual misconduct. Having abandoned lying, he refrains from lying. Having abandoned divisive speech, he refrains from divisive speech. Having abandoned harsh speech, he refrains from harsh speech. Having abandoned idle chatter, he refrains from idle chatter. Having abandoned excessive greed, he becomes generous. Having abandoned anger, he becomes one with a mind of loving kindness. Having abandoned wrong views, he becomes one who has right views."

(1) "Dear Gāmani, that noble disciple — who is thus free of excessive greed, free of anger, unconfused, alert, and mindful — meditates with the thoughts of loving kindness, focusing on the beings in the eastern direction, southern direction, western direction, and northern direction. Thus, above, below, and all around, everywhere, in its entirety, he spreads thoughts of loving kindness to the entire world — abundant, expansive, immeasurable, without hostility, and without ill will. Just as a strong conch blower easily creates a sound that resonates throughout the four directions, so too, the mind that is well developed and cultivated with loving kindness is liberated from all bad karma. Therefore, evil karma will no longer stay in that mind."

(2) "Dear Gāmani, that noble disciple — who is thus free of excessive greed, free of anger, unconfused, alert, and mindful — meditates with the thoughts of compassion... appreciative joy... and equanimity, focusing on the beings in the eastern direction, southern direction, western direction, and northern direction. Thus, above, below, and all around, everywhere, in its entirety, he spreads thoughts of loving kindness to the entire world — abundant, expansive, immeasurable, without hostility, and without ill will. Just as a strong

conch blower easily creates a sound that resonates throughout the four directions, so too, the mind that is well developed and cultivated with equanimity is liberated from all bad karma. Therefore, evil karma will no longer stay in that mind."

When the Buddha taught this Dhamma, Asibandhakaputta (blacksmith) Gāmani, a disciple of the Niganthas (the founder of Jainism) said to the Blessed One: "Excellent, Bhante! Wonderful Bhante! Just as if someone were to place upright what was overturned, to reveal what was hidden, to point out the way to one who was lost, or to carry a lamp into the dark so that those with eyes could see forms, in the same way has the Buddha— through many explanations — made the Dhamma clear to me. I go for refuge to the Buddha, to the Dhamma, and to the Sanga, the community of monks. From today onwards, may the Buddha remember me as a lay follower who has gone for refuge to the triple gem for life."

(SN 42. 8)

Chapter Two: Ghost World

2. Connected Discourses with the Monk Lakkhaṇa

2.1 Aṭṭhisaṁkhalika Suttaṁ—The Skeleton

This is how I heard. At one time, the Blessed One was staying at Rājagaha, in the Bamboo Park, the Squirrel Garden. During those days, Bhante Lakkhaṇa and Bhante Mahāmoggallāna were staying on the Gijjhakūta Mountain. One day, in the morning, Bhante Mahāmoggalāna wore his robes, took his bowl, carried his double robe and went to Bhante Lakkhaṇa and said to him, "Come, friend Lakkhana, let us go to the city of Rājagaha for alms."

"Alright, friend," Bhante Lakkhaṇa replied. Then, as he was coming down from Gijjhakūta Mountain, Bhante Mahāmoggallāna smiled at a certain place. Bhante Lakkhaṇa asked him, "Why, friend Moggallāna, did you smile?"

"Friend Lakkhaṇa, this is not the suitable time for that question. Ask me that question when we meet the Blessed One."

Then, Bhante Lakkhaṇa and Bhante Mahāmoggallāna walked for alms in the city of Rājagaha. After they returned from their alms round, they had their meal. Then, they went to the Blessed One, worshipped Him respectfully and sat down to one side. Bhante Lakkhaṇa asked Bhante Mahāmoggallāna, "This morning, while you were coming down from the Gijjhakūta Mountain, Bhante Mahāmoggallāna smiled. Why, friend Moggallāna, did you smile?"

Bhante Moggallāna replied, "This morning, friend, as I was coming down from the Gijjhakūta Mountain, I saw a skeleton moving through the air. Vultures, crows, and hawks were chasing after it. They were pecking at it between the ribs, stabbing it, and tearing it apart. The skeleton was crying out in pain. I thought then, 'It is unusual, indeed! It is amazing, indeed! That there exists such a being, that there exists such a non-human, that there exists such a life."

Then, the Blessed One said to the monks, "Monks, there are disciples who have gained the divine eye and special knowledge. They can know, see, and witness such a non-human. Monks, in the past, I, too, saw that being, but I did not speak of it. If I had spoken about it, there might have been some people who wouldn't believe my words. If they had not believed my words, it would have led them to their harm and suffering for a long time."

The Blessed One continued, "Monks, that non-human being used to be a cattle butcher in this same city of Rājagaha. As a result of that bad kamma, he was boiled in hell for many years, for many hundreds of years, for many thousands of years, for many hundreds of thousands of years. As a remaining result of that same kamma, he has been reborn as a ghost and is experiencing such terrible pain."

2.2 Mansapesi Suttaṁ—The Piece of Meat

Bhante Moggallāna said, "This morning, friend, as I was coming down from the Gijjhakūta Mountain, I saw a piece of meat moving through the air. Vultures, crows, and hawks were chasing after it. They were stabbing it and tearing it apart. The piece of meat was crying out in pain. I thought then, 'It is unusual, indeed! It is amazing, indeed! That there exists such a being, that there exists such a non-human, that there exists such a life."

Then, the Blessed One said to the monks, "Monks, there are disciples who have gained the divine eye and special knowledge. They can know, see, and witness such a non-human. Monks, in the past, I, too, saw that being, but I did not speak of it. If I had spoken about it, there might have been some people who wouldn't believe my words. If they had not believed my words, it would have led them to their harm and suffering for a long time."

The Blessed One continued, "Monks, that non-human being used to be a cattle butcher in this same city of Rājagaha. As a result of that bad kamma, he was boiled in hell for many years, for many hundreds of years, for many thousands of years, for many hundreds of thousands of years. As a remaining result of that same kamma, he has been reborn as a ghost and is experiencing such terrible pain."

2.3 Mansapinda Suttaṁ—The Lump of Meat

Bhante Moggallāna said, "This morning, friend, as I was coming down from the Gijjhakūta Mountain, I saw a lump of meat moving through the air. Vultures, crows, and hawks were chasing after it. They were stabbing it and tearing it apart. The lump of meat was crying out in pain. I thought then, 'It is unusual, indeed! It is amazing, indeed! That there exists such a being, that there exists such a non-human, that there exists such a life."

Then, the Blessed One said to the monks, "Monks, there are disciples who have gained the divine eye and special knowledge. They can know, see, and witness such a non-human. Monks, in the past, I, too, saw that being, but I did not speak of it. If I had spoken about it, there might have been some people who wouldn't believe my words. If they had not believed my words, it would have led them to their harm and suffering for a long time."

The Blessed One continued, "Monks, that non-human being used to be a poultry butcher in this same city of Rājagaha. As a result of that bad kamma, he was boiled in hell for many years, for many hundreds of years, for many thousands of years, for many hundreds of thousands of years. As a remaining result of that same kamma, he has been reborn as a ghost and is experiencing such terrible pain."

2.4 Nicchavi Suttaṁ—The Skinless Man

Bhante Moggallāna said, "This morning, friend, as I was coming down from the Gijjhakūta Mountain, I saw a skinless man moving through the air. Vultures, crows, and hawks were chasing after him. They were stabbing it and tearing it apart. The skinless man was crying out in pain. I thought then, 'It is unusual, indeed! It is amazing, indeed! That there exists such a being, that there exists such a non-human, that there exists such a life."

Then, the Blessed One said to the monks, "Monks, there are disciples who have gained the divine eye and special knowledge. They can know, see, and witness such a non-human. Monks, in the past, I, too, saw that being, but I did not speak of it. If I had spoken about it, there might have been some people who wouldn't believe my words. If they had not believed my words, it would have led them to their harm and suffering for a long time."

The Blessed One continued, "Monks, that non-human being used to be a sheep butcher in this same city of Rājagaha. As a result of that bad kamma, he was boiled in hell for many years, for many hundreds of years, for many thousands of years, for many hundreds of thousands of years. As a remaining result of that same kamma, he has been reborn as a ghost and is experiencing such terrible pain."

2.5 Asiloma Suttaṁ—The Sword-like Body Haired Man

Bhante Moggallāna said, "This morning, friend, as I was coming down from the Gijjhakūta Mountain, I saw a man with sword-like body hairs, moving through the air. Those swords kept coming out and continued stabbing his body. The man was crying out in pain. I thought then, 'It is unusual, indeed! It is amazing, indeed! That there exists such a being, that there exists such a non-human, that there exists such a life."

Then, the Blessed One said to the monks, "Monks, there are disciples who have gained the divine eye and special knowledge. They can know, see, and witness such a non-human. Monks, in the past, I, too, saw that being, but I did not speak of it. If I had spoken about it, there might have been some people who wouldn't believe my words. If they had not believed my words, it would have led them to their harm and suffering for a long time."

The Blessed One continued, "Monks, that non-human being used to be a pig butcher in this same city of Rājagaha. As a result of that bad kamma, he was boiled in hell for many years, for many hundreds of years, for many thousands of years, for many hundreds of thousands of years. As a remaining result of that same kamma, he has been reborn as a ghost and is experiencing such terrible pain."

2.6 Sattiloma Suttaṁ— The Curved Knife-like Body Haired Man

Bhante Moggallāna said, "This morning, friend, as I was coming down from the Gijjhakūta Mountain, I saw a man with curved knife-like body hairs moving through the air. Those knives kept coming out and continued stabbing his body. The man was crying out in pain. I thought then, 'It is unusual, indeed! It is amazing, indeed! That there exists such a being, that there exists such a non-human, that there exists such a life."

Then, the Blessed One said to the monks, "Monks, there are disciples who have gained the divine eye and special knowledge. They can know, see, and witness such a non-human. Monks, in the past, I, too, saw that being, but I did not speak of it. If I had spoken about it, there might have been some people who wouldn't believe my words. If they had not believed my words, it would have led them to their harm and suffering for a long time."

The Blessed One continued, "Monks, that non-human being used to be a deer hunter in this same city of Rājagaha. As a result of that bad kamma, he was boiled in hell for many years, for many hundreds of years, for many thousands of years, for many hundreds of thousands of years. As a remaining result of that same kamma, he has been reborn as a ghost and is experiencing such terrible pain."

2.7 Usuloma Suttaṁ—The Arrow-like Body Haired Man

Bhante Moggallāna said, "This morning, friend, as I was coming down from the Gijjhakūta Mountain, I saw a man with arrow-like body hairs, moving through the air. Those arrows kept coming out and continued stabbing his body. The man was crying out in pain. I thought then, 'It is unusual, indeed! It is amazing, indeed! That there exists such a being, that there exists such a non-human, that there exists such a life."

Then, the Blessed One said to the monks, "Monks, there are disciples who have gained the divine eye and special knowledge. They can know, see, and witness such a non-human. Monks, in the past, I, too, saw that being, but I did not speak of it. If I had spoken about it, there might have been some people who wouldn't believe my words. If they had not believed my words, it would have led them to their harm and suffering for a long time."

The Blessed One continued, "Monks, that non-human being used to be a torturer in this same city of Rājagaha. As a result of that bad kamma, he was boiled in hell for many years, for many hundreds of years, for many thousands of years, for many hundreds of thousands of years. As a remaining result of that same kamma, he has been reborn as a ghost and is experiencing such terrible pain."

2.8 Suciloma Suttaṁ—The Needle-like Body Haired Man

Bhante Moggallāna said, "This morning, friend, as I was coming down from the Gijjhakūta Mountain, I saw a man with needle-like body hairs moving through the air. Those needles kept coming out and continued stabbing his body. The man was crying out in pain. I thought then, 'It is unusual, indeed! It is amazing, indeed! That there exists such a being, that there exists such a non-human, that there exists such a life."

Then, the Blessed One said to the monks, "Monks, there are disciples who have gained the divine eye and special knowledge. They can know, see, and witness such a non-human. Monks, in the past, I, too, saw that being, but I did not speak of it. If I had spoken about it, there might have been some people who wouldn't believe my words. If they had not believed my words, it would have led them to their harm and suffering for a long time."

The Blessed One continued, "Monks, that non-human being used to be an evil driver in this same city of Rājagaha. As a result of that bad kamma, he was boiled in hell for many years, for many hundreds of years, for many thousands of years, for many hundreds of thousands of years. As a remaining result of that same kamma, he has been reborn as a ghost and is experiencing such terrible pain."

2.9 Dutiya Suciloma Suttaṁ—The Needle-like Body Haired Man (2)

Bhante Moggallāna said, "This morning, friend, as I was coming down from the Gijjhakūta Mountain, I saw a man with needle-like body hairs moving through the air. Those needles kept coming out and continued stabbing his body. The man was crying out in pain. I thought then, 'It is unusual, indeed! It is amazing, indeed! That there exists such a being, that there exists such a non-human, that there exists such a life."

Then, the Blessed One said to the monks, "Monks, there are disciples who have gained the divine eye and special knowledge. They can know, see, and witness such a non-human. Monks, in the past, I, too, saw that being, but I did not speak of it. If I had spoken about it, there might have been some people who wouldn't believe my words. If they had not believed my words, it would have led them to their harm and suffering for a long time."

The Blessed One continued, "Monks, that non-human being used to be a slanderer who broke friendships using divisive speech in this same city of Rājagaha. As a result of that bad kamma, he was boiled in hell for many years, for many hundreds of years, for many thousands of years, for many hundreds of thousands of years. As a remaining result of that same kamma, he has been reborn as a ghost and is experiencing such terrible pain."

2.10 Kumbhanda Suttaṁ—The Pot-like Testicles

Bhante Moggallāna said, "This morning, friend, as I was coming down from the Gijjhakūta Mountain, I saw a man with pot-like testicles moving through the air. When he walked, he had to lift his testicles onto his shoulders and when he sat down he sat on top of his testicles. Vultures, crows, and hawks were chasing after it. They were stabbing it and tearing it apart. The man was crying out in pain. I thought then, 'It is unusual, indeed! It is amazing, indeed! That there exists such a being, that there exists such a non-human, that there exists such a life."

Then, the Blessed One said to the monks, "Monks, there are disciples who have gained the divine eye and special knowledge. They can know, see, and witness such a non-human. Monks, in the past, I, too, saw that being, but I did not speak of it. If I had spoken about it, there might have been some people who wouldn't believe my words. If they had not believed my words, it would have led them to their harm and suffering for a long time."

The Blessed One continued, "Monks, that non-human being used to be an evil judge, in this same city of Rājagaha. As a result of that bad kamma, he was boiled in hell for many years, for many hundreds of years, for many thousands of years, for many hundreds of thousands of years. As a remaining result of that same kamma, he has been reborn as a ghost and is experiencing such terrible pain."

2.11 Guthakupa Suttaṁ—The Pit of Dung

Bhante Moggallāna said, "This morning, friend, as I was coming down from the Gijjhakūta Mountain, I saw a man with his head submerged in a pit of dung. The man was crying out in pain. I thought then, 'It is unusual, indeed! It is amazing, indeed! That there exists such a being, that there exists such a non-human, that there exists such a life."

Then, the Blessed One said to the monks, "Monks, there are disciples who have gained the divine eye and special knowledge. They can know, see, and witness such a non-human. Monks, in the past, I, too, saw that being, but I did not speak of it. If I had spoken about it, there might have been some people who wouldn't believe my words. If they had not believed my words, it would have led them to their harm and suffering for a long time."

The Blessed One continued, "Monks, that non-human being used to be a man who engaged in sexual misconduct with others wives, in this same city of Rājagaha. As a result of that bad kamma, he was boiled in hell for many years, for many hundreds of years, for many thousands of years, for many hundreds of thousands of years. As a remaining result of that same kamma, he has been reborn as a ghost and is experiencing such terrible pain."

2.12 Guthakhadi Suttaṁ—The Dung Eater

Bhante Moggallāna said, "This morning, friend, as I was coming down from the Gijjhakūta Mountain, I saw a man with his head submerged in a pit of dung, devouring dung with his both hands. The man was crying out in pain. I thought then, 'It is unusual, indeed! It is amazing, indeed! That there exists such a being, that there exists such a non-human, that there exists such a life.'"

Then, the Blessed One said to the monks, "Monks, there are disciples who have gained the divine eye and special knowledge. They can know, see, and witness such a non-human. Monks, in the past, I, too, saw that being, but I did not speak of it. If I had spoken about it, there might have been some people who wouldn't believe my words. If they had not believed my words, it would have led them to their harm and suffering for a long time."

The Blessed One continued, "Monks, that non-human being was a brāhamin in the time of the Kassapa Buddha in this same city of Rājagaha. One day, he invited the monks for a meal. He filled rice pots with dung and called the monks saying, 'Sirs, eat as much as you want from this and take the rest away with you!' As a result of that bad kamma, he was boiled in hell for many years, for many hundreds of years, for many thousands of years, for many hundreds of thousands of years. As a remaining result of that same kamma, he has been reborn as a ghost and is experiencing such terrible pain."

2.13 Nicchavitthi Suttaṁ—The Skinless Woman

Bhante Moggallāna said, "This morning, friend, as I was coming down from the Gijjhakūta Mountain, I saw a skinless woman moving through the air. Vultures, crows, and hawks were chasing after it. They were stabbing it and tearing it apart. The woman was crying out in pain. I thought then, 'It is unusual, indeed! It is amazing, indeed! That there exists such a being, that there exists such a non-human, that there exists such a life."

Then, the Blessed One said to the monks, "Monks, there are disciples who have gained the divine eye and special knowledge. They can know, see, and witness such a non-human. Monks, in the past, I, too, saw that being, but I did not speak of it. If I had spoken about it, there might have been some people who wouldn't believe my words. If they had not believed my words, it would have led them to their harm and suffering for a long time."

The Blessed One continued, "Monks, that non-human being was a prostitute in this same city of Rājagaha. As a result of that bad kamma, she was boiled in hell for many years, for many hundreds of years, for many thousands of years, for many hundreds of thousands of years. As a remaining result of that same kamma, she has been reborn as a ghost and is experiencing such terrible pain."

2.14 Maṁgulitthi Suttaṁ—The Ugly Woman

Bhante Moggallāna said, "This morning, friend, as I was coming down from the Gijjhakūta Mountain, I saw a woman, foul smelling and ugly, moving through the air. Vultures, crows, and hawks were chasing after it. They were stabbing it and tearing it apart. The woman was crying out in pain. I thought then, 'It is unusual, indeed! It is amazing, indeed! That there exists such a being, that there exists such a non-human, that there exists such a life."

Then, the Blessed One said to the monks, "Monks, there are disciples who have gained the divine eye and special knowledge. They can know, see, and witness such a non-human. Monks, in the past, I, too, saw that being, but I did not speak of it. If I had spoken about it, there might have been some people who wouldn't believe my words. If they had not believed my words, it would have led them to their harm and suffering for a long time."

The Blessed One continued, "Monks, that non-human being was an evil fortune-teller in this same city of Rājagaha. As a result of that bad kamma, she was boiled in hell for many years, for many hundreds of years, for many thousands of years, for many hundreds of thousands of years. As a remaining result of that same kamma, she has been reborn as a ghost and is experiencing such terrible pain."

2.15 Okilinī Suttaṁ—The Scorched Woman

Bhante Moggallāna said, "This morning, friend, as I was coming down from the Gijjhakūta Mountain, I saw a woman with her body roasting, sweaty, scorching, and moving through the air. The woman was crying out in pain. I thought then, 'It is unusual, indeed! It is amazing, indeed! That there exists such a being, that there exists such a non-human, that there exists such a life.'"

Then, the Blessed One said to the monks, "Monks, there are disciples who have gained the divine eye and special knowledge. They can know, see, and witness such a non-human. Monks, in the past, I, too, saw that being, but I did not speak of it. If I had spoken about it, there might have been some people who wouldn't believe my words. If they had not believed my words, it would have led them to their harm and suffering for a long time."

The Blessed One continued, "Monks, that non-human being was the chief queen of the King Kaliṅga. Out of jealousy, she poured a plate of burning coal over another wife of the king. As a result of that bad kamma, she was boiled in hell for many years, for many hundreds of years, for many thousands of years, for many hundreds of thousands of years. As a remaining result of that same kamma, she has been reborn as a ghost and is experiencing such terrible pain."

2.16 Asīsaka Suttaṁ—The Headless Body

Bhante Moggallāna said, "This morning, friend, as I was coming down from the Gijjhakūṭa Mountain, I saw a headless body moving through the air; its eyes and mouth were on its chest. Vultures, crows, and hawks were chasing after it. They were stabbing it and tearing it apart. It was crying out in pain. I thought then, 'It is unusual, indeed! It is amazing, indeed! That there exists such a being, that there exists such a non-human, that there exists such a life.'"

Then, the Blessed One said to the monks, "Monks, there are disciples who have gained the divine eye and special knowledge. They can know, see, and witness such a non-human. Monks, in the past, I, too, saw that being, but I did not speak of it. If I had spoken about it, there might have been some people who wouldn't believe my words. If they had not believed my words, it would have led them to their harm and suffering for a long time."

The Blessed One continued, "Monks, that non-human being used to be a killer of thieves named Hārika in this same city of Rājagaha. As a result of that bad kamma, he was boiled in hell for many years, for many hundreds of years, for many thousands of years, for many hundreds of thousands of years. As a remaining result of that same kamma, he has been reborn as a ghost and is experiencing such terrible pain."

2.17 Bhikkhu Suttaṁ—The Evil Monk

Bhante Moggallāna said, "This morning, friend, as I was coming down from the Gijjhakūta Mountain, I saw a monk moving through the air. His robe, bowl, waistband, and body were burning, blazing, and flaming. The monk was crying out in pain. I thought then, 'It is unusual, indeed! It is amazing, indeed! That there exists such a being, that there exists such a non-human, that there exists such a life."

Then, the Blessed One said to the monks, "Monks, there are disciples who have gained the divine eye and special knowledge. They can know, see, and witness such a non-human. Monks, in the past, I, too, saw that being, but I did not speak of it. If I had spoken about it, there might have been some people who wouldn't believe my words. If they had not believed my words, it would have led them to their harm and suffering for a long time."

The Blessed One continued, "Monks, that non-human being had been an evil monk in the Kassapa Buddha's time. As a result of that bad kamma, he was boiled in hell for many years, for many hundreds of years, for many thousands of years, for many hundreds of thousands of years. As a remaining result of that same kamma, he has been reborn as a ghost and is experiencing such terrible pain."

2.18 Bhikkhunī Suttaṁ—The Evil Nun

Bhante Moggallāna said, "This morning, friend, as I was coming down from the Gijjhakūta Mountain, I saw a nun moving through the air. Her robe, bowl, waistband, and body were burning, blazing, and flaming. The nun was crying out in pain. I thought then, 'It is unusual, indeed! It is amazing, indeed! That there exists such a being, that there exists such a non-human, that there exists such a life."

Then, the Blessed One said to the monks, "Monks, there are disciples who have gained the divine eye and special knowledge. They can know, see, and witness such a non-human. Monks, in the past, I, too, saw that being, but I did not speak of it. If I had spoken about it, there might have been some people who wouldn't believe my words. If they had not believed my words, it would have led them to their harm and suffering for a long time."

The Blessed One continued, "Monks, that non-human being had been an evil nun in the Kassapa Buddha's time. As a result of that bad kamma, she was boiled in hell for many years, for many hundreds of years, for many thousands of years, for many hundreds of thousands of years. As a remaining result of that same kamma, she has been reborn as a ghost and is experiencing such terrible pain."

2.19 Sikkhamānā Suttaṁ—The Trainee-Nun

Bhante Moggallāna said, "This morning, friend, as I was coming down from the Gijjhakūta Mountain, I saw a trainee-nun moving through the air. Her robe, bowl, waistband, and body were burning, blazing, and flaming. She was crying out in pain. I thought then, 'It is unusual, indeed! It is amazing, indeed! That there exists such a being, that there exists such a non-human, that there exists such a life."

Then, the Blessed One said to the monks, "Monks, there are disciples who have gained the divine eye and special knowledge. They can know, see, and witness such a non-human. Monks, in the past, I, too, saw that being, but I did not speak of it. If I had spoken about it, there might have been some people who wouldn't believe my words. If they had not believed my words, it would have led them to their harm and suffering for a long time."

The Blessed One continued, "Monks, that non-human being had been an evil trainee-nun in the Kassapa Buddha's time. As a result of that bad kamma, she was boiled in hell for many years, for many hundreds of years, for many thousands of years, for many hundreds of thousands of years. As a remaining result of that same kamma, she has been reborn as a ghost and is experiencing such terrible pain."

2.20 Sāmanera Suttaṁ—The Novice Monk

Bhante Moggallāna said, "This morning, friend, as I was coming down from the Gijjhakūta Mountain, I saw a novice-monk moving through the air. His robe, bowl, waistband, and body were burning, blazing, and flaming. The monk was crying out in pain. I thought then, 'It is unusual, indeed! It is amazing, indeed! That there exists such a being, that there exists such a non-human, that there exists such a life."

Then, the Blessed One said to the monks, "Monks, there are disciples who have gained the divine eye and special knowledge. They can know, see, and witness such a non-human. Monks, in the past, I, too, saw that being, but I did not speak of it. If I had spoken about it, there might have been some people who wouldn't believe my words. If they had not believed my words, it would have led them to their harm and suffering for a long time."

The Blessed One continued, "Monks, that non-human being had been an evil novice-monk in the Kassapa Buddha's time. As a result of that bad kamma, he was boiled in hell for many years, for many hundreds of years, for many thousands of years, for many hundreds of thousands of years. As a remaining result of that same kamma, he has been reborn as a ghost and is experiencing such terrible pain."

2.21 Sāmanerī Suttaṁ—The Novice Nun

Bhante Moggallāna said, "This morning, friend, as I was coming down from the Gijjhakūta Mountain, I saw a novice-nun moving through the air. Her robe, bowl, waistband, and body were burning, blazing, and flaming. She was crying out in pain. I thought then, 'It is unusual, indeed! It is amazing, indeed! That there exists such a being, that there exists such a non-human, that there exists such a life."

Then, the Blessed One said to the monks, "Monks, there are disciples who have gained the divine eye and special knowledge. They can know, see, and witness such a non-human. Monks, in the past, I, too, saw that being, but I did not speak of it. If I had spoken about it, there might have been some people who wouldn't believe my words. If they had not believed my words, it would have led them to their harm and suffering for a long time."

The Blessed One continued, "Monks, that non-human being had been an evil novice-nun in the Kassapa Buddha's time. As a result of that bad kamma, she was boiled in hell for many years, for many hundreds of years, for many thousands of years, for many hundreds of thousands of years. As a remaining result of that same kamma, she has been reborn as a ghost and is experiencing such terrible pain."

Chapter Three:

The Five Destinations of Beings

3.1 Manussa Cuti Suttaṁ—Passing Away as Humans

One day, the Blessed One took up a little bit of soil in his fingernail and asked the monks "What do you think, monks, which is more: the little bit of soil in my fingernail or the great earth?"

"Bhante, the great earth is more. The little bit of soil that the Blessed One has taken up in his fingernail is very small. Compared to the great earth, the little bit of soil that the Blessed One has taken up in his fingernail is not knowable, is beyond comparison, and not even an amount of a fraction."

(1) "So too, monks, when human beings pass away, the amount of beings reborn as humans again in their next life is extremely few. However, when human beings pass away, the amount of beings reborn in hell in their next life is extremely large. What is the reason for this? It is because, monks, they have not understood The Four Noble Truths. What are those Four Noble Truths?

The noble truth of suffering, the noble truth of the cause of suffering, the noble truth of the end of suffering, and the noble truth of the path to the end of suffering."

"Therefore, monks, you must put an effort to understand 'This is suffering.' You must put an effort to understand 'This is the cause of suffering.' You must put an effort to understand 'This is the end of suffering.' You must put an effort to understand 'This is the path to the end of suffering.'"

(2) "So too, monks, when human beings pass away, the amount of beings reborn as humans again in their next life is extremely few. However, when human beings pass away, the amount of beings reborn as animals in their next life is extremely large. What is the reason for this? It is because, monks, they have not understood The Four Noble Truths. What are those Four Noble Truths?

The noble truth of suffering, the noble truth of the cause of suffering, the noble truth of the end of suffering, and the noble truth of the path to the end of suffering."

"Therefore, monks, you must put an effort to understand 'This is suffering.' You must put an effort to understand 'This is the cause of suffering.' You must put an effort to understand 'This is the end of suffering.' You must put an effort to understand 'This is the path to the end of suffering.'"

(3) "So too, monks, when human beings pass away, the amount of beings reborn as humans again in their next life is extremely few. However, when human beings pass away, the amount of beings reborn as ghosts in their next life is extremely large. What is the reason for this? It is because, monks, they have not understood The Four Noble Truths. What are those Four Noble Truths?

The noble truth of suffering, the noble truth of the cause of suffering, the noble truth of the end of suffering, and the noble truth of the path to the end of suffering."

"Therefore, monks, you must put an effort to understand 'This is suffering.' You must put an effort to understand 'This is the cause of suffering.' You must put an effort to understand 'This is the end of suffering.' You must put an effort to understand 'This is the path to the end of suffering.'"

(4) "So too, monks, when human beings pass away, the amount of beings reborn as gods again in their next life is extremely few. However, when human beings pass away, the amount of beings reborn in hell in their next life is extremely large. What is the reason for this? It is because, monks, they have not understood The Four Noble Truths. What are those Four Noble Truths?

The noble truth of suffering, the noble truth of the cause of suffering, the noble truth of the end of suffering, and the noble truth of the path to the end of suffering."

"Therefore, monks, you must put an effort to understand 'This is suffering.' You must put an effort to understand 'This is the cause of suffering.' You must put an effort to understand 'This is the end of suffering.' You must put an effort to understand 'This is the path to the end of suffering."

(5) "So too, monks, when human beings pass away, the amount of beings reborn as gods again in their next life is extremely few. However, when human beings pass away, the amount of beings reborn as animals in their next life is extremely large. What is the reason for this? It is because, monks, they have not understood The Four Noble Truths. What are those Four Noble Truths?

The noble truth of suffering, the noble truth of the cause of suffering, the noble truth of the end of suffering, and the noble truth of the path to the end of suffering."

"Therefore, monks, you must put an effort to understand 'This is suffering.' You must put an effort to understand 'This is the cause of suffering.' You must put an effort to understand 'This is the end of suffering.' You must put an effort to understand 'This is the path to the end of suffering."

(6) "So too, monks, when human beings pass away, the amount of beings reborn as gods again in their next life is extremely few. However, when human beings pass away, the amount of beings reborn as ghosts in their next life is extremely large. What is the reason for this? It is because, monks, they have not understood The Four Noble Truths. What are those Four Noble Truths?

The noble truth of suffering, the noble truth of the cause of suffering, the noble truth of the end of suffering, and the noble truth of the path to the end of suffering."

"Therefore, monks, you must put an effort to understand 'This is suffering.' You must put an effort to understand 'This is the cause of suffering.' You must put an effort to understand 'This is the end of suffering.' You must put an effort to understand 'This is the path to the end of suffering."

3.2 Deva Cuti Suttaṁ—Passing Away as Gods

One day, the Blessed One took up a little bit of soil in his fingernail and asked the monks "What do you think, monks, which is more: the little bit of soil in my fingernail or the great earth?"

"Bhante, the great earth is more. The little bit of soil that the Blessed One has taken up in his fingernail is very small. Compared to the great earth, the little bit of soil that the Blessed One has taken up in his fingernail is not knowable, is beyond comparison, and not even an amount of a fraction."

(1) "So too, monks, when gods pass away, the amount of beings reborn as gods again in their next life is extremely few. However, when gods pass away, the amount of gods

reborn in hell in their next life is extremely large. What is the reason for this? It is because, monks, they have not understood The Four Noble Truths. What are those Four Noble Truths?

The noble truth of suffering, the noble truth of the cause of suffering, the noble truth of the end of suffering, and the noble truth of the path to the end of suffering."

"Therefore, monks, you must put an effort to understand 'This is suffering.' You must put an effort to understand 'This is the cause of suffering.' You must put an effort to understand 'This is the end of suffering.' You must put an effort to understand 'This is the path to the end of suffering.'"

(2) "So too, monks, when gods pass away, the amount of beings reborn as gods again in their next life is extremely few. However, when gods pass away, the amount of gods reborn as animals in their next life is extremely large. What is the reason for this? It is because, monks, they have not understood The Four Noble Truths. What are those Four Noble Truths?

The noble truth of suffering, the noble truth of the cause of suffering, the noble truth of the end of suffering, and the noble truth of the path to the end of suffering."

"Therefore, monks, you must put an effort to understand 'This is suffering.' You must put an effort to understand 'This is the cause of suffering.' You must put an effort to understand 'This is the end of suffering.' You must put an effort to understand 'This is the path to the end of suffering.'"

(3) "So too, monks, when gods pass away, the amount of beings reborn as gods again in their next life is extremely few. However, when gods pass away, the amount of gods

reborn as ghosts in their next life is extremely large. What is the reason for this? It is because, monks, they have not understood The Four Noble Truths. What are those Four Noble Truths?

The noble truth of suffering, the noble truth of the cause of suffering, the noble truth of the end of suffering, and the noble truth of the path to the end of suffering."

"Therefore, monks, you must put an effort to understand 'This is suffering.' You must put an effort to understand 'This is the cause of suffering.' You must put an effort to understand 'This is the end of suffering.' You must put an effort to understand 'This is the path to the end of suffering."

(4) "So too, monks, when gods pass away, the amount of beings reborn as humans again in their next life is extremely few. However, when gods pass away, the amount of gods reborn in hell in their next life is extremely large. What is the reason for this? It is because, monks, they have not understood The Four Noble Truths. What are those Four Noble Truths?

The noble truth of suffering, the noble truth of the cause of suffering, the noble truth of the end of suffering, and the noble truth of the path to the end of suffering."

"Therefore, monks, you must put an effort to understand 'This is suffering.' You must put an effort to understand 'This is the cause of suffering.' You must put an effort to understand 'This is the end of suffering.' You must put an effort to understand 'This is the path to the end of suffering."

(5) "So too, monks, when gods pass away, the amount of beings reborn as humans again in their next life is extremely few. However, when gods pass away, the amount of gods

reborn as animals in their next life is extremely large. What is the reason for this? It is because, monks, they have not understood The Four Noble Truths. What are those Four Noble Truths?

The noble truth of suffering, the noble truth of the cause of suffering, the noble truth of the end of suffering, and the noble truth of the path to the end of suffering."

"Therefore, monks, you must put an effort to understand 'This is suffering.' You must put an effort to understand 'This is the cause of suffering.' You must put an effort to understand 'This is the end of suffering.' You must put an effort to understand 'This is the path to the end of suffering."

(6) "So too, monks, when gods pass away, the amount of beings reborn as humans again in their next life is extremely few. However, when gods pass away, the amount of gods reborn as ghosts in their next life is extremely large. What is the reason for this? It is because, monks, they have not understood The Four Noble Truths. What are those Four Noble Truths?

The noble truth of suffering, the noble truth of the cause of suffering, the noble truth of the end of suffering, and the noble truth of the path to the end of suffering."

"Therefore, monks, you must put an effort to understand 'This is suffering.' You must put an effort to understand 'This is the cause of suffering.' You must put an effort to understand 'This is the end of suffering.' You must put an effort to understand 'This is the path to the end of suffering."

3.3 Niraya Cuti Suttaṁ—Passing Away from Hell

One day, the Blessed One took up a little bit of soil in his fingernail and asked the monks "What do you think, monks, which is more: the little bit of soil in my fingernail or the great earth?"

"Bhante, the great earth is more. The little bit of soil that the Blessed One has taken up in his fingernail is very small. Compared to the great earth, the little bit of soil that the Blessed One has taken up in his fingernail is not knowable, is beyond comparison, and not even an amount of a fraction."

(1) "So too, monks, when hell beings pass away, the amount of beings reborn as humans again in their next life is extremely few. However, when hell beings pass away, the amount of beings reborn as hell beings in their next life is extremely large. What is the reason for this? it is because, monks, they have not understood The Four Noble Truths. What are those Four Noble Truths?

The noble truth of suffering, the noble truth of the cause of suffering, the noble truth of the end of suffering, and the noble truth of the path to the end of suffering."

"Therefore, monks, you must put an effort to understand 'This is suffering.' You must put an effort to understand 'This is the cause of suffering.' You must put an effort to understand 'This is the end of suffering.' You must put an effort to understand 'This is the path to the end of suffering.'"

(2) "So too, monks, when hell beings pass away, the amount of beings reborn as humans again in their next life is extremely few. However, when hell beings pass away, the amount of beings who are reborn as animals in their next life

is extremely large. What is the reason for this? It is because, monks, they have not understood The Four Noble Truths. What are those Four Noble Truths?

The noble truth of suffering, the noble truth of the cause of suffering, the noble truth of the end of suffering, and the noble truth of the path to the end of suffering."

"Therefore, monks, you must put an effort to understand 'This is suffering.' You must put an effort to understand 'This is the cause of suffering.' You must put an effort to understand 'This is the end of suffering.' You must put an effort to understand 'This is the path to the end of suffering."

(3) "So too, monks, when hell beings pass away, the amount of beings who are reborn as humans again in their next life is extremely few. However, when hell beings pass away, the amount of beings reborn as ghosts in their next life is extremely large. What is the reason for this? It is because, monks, they have not understood The Four Noble Truths. What are those Four Noble Truths?

The noble truth of suffering, the noble truth of the cause of suffering, the noble truth of the end of suffering, and the noble truth of the path to the end of suffering."

"Therefore, monks, you must put an effort to understand 'This is suffering.' You must put an effort to understand 'This is the cause of suffering.' You must put an effort to understand 'This is the end of suffering.' You must put an effort to understand 'This is the path to the end of suffering."

(4) "So too, monks, when hell beings pass away, the amount of beings reborn as gods again in their next life is extremely few. However, when hell beings pass away, the amount of beings reborn as hell beings in their next life is

extremely large. What is the reason for this? It is because, monks, they have not understood The Four Noble Truths. What are those Four Noble Truths?

The noble truth of suffering, the noble truth of the cause of suffering, the noble truth of the end of suffering, and the noble truth of the path to the end of suffering."

"Therefore, monks, you must put an effort to understand 'This is suffering.' You must put an effort to understand 'This is the cause of suffering.' You must put an effort to understand 'This is the end of suffering.' You must put an effort to understand 'This is the path to the end of suffering.'

(5) "So too, monks, when hell beings pass away, the amount of beings reborn as gods again in their next life is extremely few. However, when hell beings pass away, the amount of beings reborn as animals in their next life is extremely large. What is the reason for this? It is because, monks, they have not understood The Four Noble Truths. What are those Four Noble Truths?

The noble truth of suffering, the noble truth of the cause of suffering, the noble truth of the end of suffering, and the noble truth of the path to the end of suffering."

"Therefore, monks, you must put an effort to understand 'This is suffering.' You must put an effort to understand 'This is the cause of suffering.' You must put an effort to understand 'This is the end of suffering.' You must put an effort to understand 'This is the path to the end of suffering."

(6) "So too, monks, when hell beings pass away, the amount of beings reborn as gods again in their next life is extremely few. However, when hell beings pass away, the amount of beings reborn as ghosts in their next life is

extremely large. What is the reason for this? It is because, monks, they have not understood The Four Noble Truths. What are those Four Noble Truths?

The noble truth of suffering, the noble truth of the cause of suffering, the noble truth of the end of suffering, and the noble truth of the path to the end of suffering."

"Therefore, monks, you must put an effort to understand 'This is suffering.' You must put an effort to understand 'This is the cause of suffering.' You must put an effort to understand 'This is the end of suffering.' You must put an effort to understand 'This is the path to the end of suffering.'"

3.4 Tiracchāna Cuti Suttaṁ—Passing Away as Animals

One day, the Blessed One took up a little bit of soil in his fingernail and asked the monks "What do you think, monks, which is more: the little bit of soil in my fingernail or the great earth?"

"Bhante, the great earth is more. The little bit of soil that the Blessed One has taken up in his fingernail is very small. Compared to the great earth, the little bit of soil that the Blessed One has taken up in his fingernail is not knowable, is beyond comparison, and not even an amount of a fraction."

(1) "So too, monks, when animals pass away, the amount of beings reborn as humans again in their next life is extremely few. However, when animals pass away, the amount of beings who are reborn as hell beings in their next life is extremely large. What is the reason for this? It is because, monks, they have not understood The Four Noble Truths. What are those Four Noble Truths?

The noble truth of suffering, the noble truth of the cause of suffering, the noble truth of the end of suffering, and the noble truth of the path to the end of suffering."

"Therefore, monks, you must put an effort to understand 'This is suffering.' You must put an effort to understand 'This is the cause of suffering.' You must put an effort to understand 'This is the end of suffering.' You must put an effort to understand 'This is the path to the end of suffering."

(2) "So too, monks, when animals pass away, the amount of beings reborn as humans again in their next life is extremely few. However, when animals pass away, the amount of beings reborn as animals in their next life is extremely large. What is the reason for this? It is because, monks, they have not understood The Four Noble Truths. What are those Four Noble Truths?

The noble truth of suffering, the noble truth of the cause of suffering, the noble truth of the end of suffering ,and the noble truth of the path to the end of suffering."

"Therefore, monks, you must put an effort to understand 'This is suffering.' You must put an effort to understand 'This is the cause of suffering.' You must put an effort to understand 'This is the end of suffering.' You must put an effort to understand 'This is the path to the end of suffering."

(3) "So too, monks, when animals pass away, the amount of beings reborn as humans again in their next life is extremely few. However, when animals pass away, the amount of beings reborn as ghosts in their next life is extremely large. What is the reason for this? It is because, monks, they have not understood The Four Noble Truths. What are those Four Noble Truths?

The noble truth of suffering, the noble truth of the cause of suffering, the noble truth of the end of suffering, and the noble truth of the path to the end of suffering."

"Therefore, monks, you must put an effort to understand 'This is suffering.' You must put an effort to understand 'This is the cause of suffering.' You must put an effort to understand 'This is the end of suffering.' You must put an effort to understand 'This is the path to the end of suffering.'"

(4) "So too, monks, when animals pass away, the amount of beings reborn as gods again in their next life is extremely few. However, when animals pass away, the amount of beings reborn as hell beings in their next life is extremely large. What is the reason for this? It is because, monks, they have not understood The Four Noble Truths. What are those Four Noble Truths?

The noble truth of suffering, the noble truth of the cause of suffering, the noble truth of the end of suffering, and the noble truth of the path to the end of suffering."

"Therefore, monks, you must put an effort to understand 'This is suffering.' You must put an effort to understand 'This is the cause of suffering.' You must put an effort to understand 'This is the end of suffering.' You must put an effort to understand 'This is the path to the end of suffering.'"

(5) "So too, monks, when animals pass away, the amount of beings reborn as gods again in their next life is extremely few. However, when animals pass away, the amount of beings reborn as animals in their next life is extremely large. What is the reason for this? It is because, monks, they have not understood The Four Noble Truths. What are those Four Noble Truths?

The noble truth of suffering, the noble truth of the cause of suffering, the noble truth of the end of suffering, and the noble truth of the path to the end of suffering."

"Therefore, monks, you must put an effort to understand 'This is suffering.' You must put an effort to understand 'This is the cause of suffering.' You must put an effort to understand 'This is the end of suffering.' You must put an effort to understand 'This is the path to the end of suffering."

(6) "So too, monks, when animals pass away, the amount of beings reborn as gods again in their next life is extremely few. However, when animals pass away, the amount of beings reborn as ghosts in their next life is extremely large. What is the reason for this? It is because, monks, they have not understood The Four Noble Truths. What are those Four Noble Truths?

The noble truth of suffering, the noble truth of the cause of suffering, the noble truth of the end of suffering, and the noble truth of the path to the end of suffering."

"Therefore, monks, you must put an effort to understand 'This is suffering.' You must put an effort to understand 'This is the cause of suffering.' You must put an effort to understand 'This is the end of suffering.' You must put an effort to understand 'This is the path to the end of suffering."

3.5 Petti Cuti Suttaṁ—Passing Away as Ghosts

One day, the Blessed One took up a little bit of soil in his fingernail and asked the monks "What do you think, monks, which is more: the little bit of soil in my fingernail or the great earth?"

"Bhante, the great earth is more. The little bit of soil that the Blessed One has taken up in his fingernail is very small. Compared to the great earth, the little bit of soil that the Blessed One has taken up in his fingernail is not knowable, is beyond comparison, and not even an amount of a fraction."

(1) "So too, monks, when ghosts pass away, the amount of beings reborn as humans again in their next life is extremely few. However, when ghosts pass away, the amount of beings reborn as hell beings in their next life is extremely large. What is the reason for this? It is because, monks, they have not understood The Four Noble Truths. What are those Four Noble Truths?

The noble truth of suffering, the noble truth of the cause of suffering, the noble truth of the end of suffering, and the noble truth of the path to the end of suffering."

"Therefore, monks, you must put an effort to understand 'This is suffering.' You must put an effort to understand 'This is the cause of suffering.' You must put an effort to understand 'This is the end of suffering.' You must put an effort to understand 'This is the path to the end of suffering.'"

(2) "So too, monks, when ghosts pass away, the amount of beings reborn as humans again in their next life is extremely few. However, when ghosts pass away, the amount of beings reborn as animals in their next life is extremely large. What is the reason for this? It is because, monks, they have not understood The Four Noble Truths. What are those Four Noble Truths?

The noble truth of suffering, the noble truth of the cause of suffering, the noble truth of the end of suffering, and the noble truth of the path to the end of suffering."

"Therefore, monks, you must put an effort to understand 'This is suffering.' You must put an effort to understand 'This is the cause of suffering.' You must put an effort to understand 'This is the end of suffering.' You must put an effort to understand 'This is the path to the end of suffering.'"

(3) "So too, monks, when ghosts pass away, the amount of beings reborn as humans again in their next life is extremely few. However, when ghosts pass away, the amount of beings reborn as ghosts in their next life is extremely large. What is the reason for this? It is because, monks, they have not understood The Four Noble Truths. What are those Four Noble Truths?

The noble truth of suffering, the noble truth of the cause of suffering, the noble truth of the end of suffering, and the noble truth of the path to the end of suffering."

"Therefore, monks, you must put an effort to understand 'This is suffering.' You must put an effort to understand 'This is the cause of suffering.' You must put an effort to understand 'This is the end of suffering.' You must put an effort to understand 'This is the path to the end of suffering.'"

(4) "So too, monks, when ghosts pass away, the amount of beings reborn as gods again in their next life is extremely few. However, when ghosts pass away, the amount of beings reborn as hell beings in their next life is extremely large. What is the reason for this? It is because, monks, they have not understood The Four Noble Truths. What are those Four Noble Truths?

The noble truth of suffering, the noble truth of the cause of suffering, the noble truth of the end of suffering, and the noble truth of the path to the end of suffering."

"Therefore, monks, you must put an effort to understand 'This is suffering.' You must put an effort to understand 'This is the cause of suffering.' You must put an effort to understand 'This is the end of suffering.' You must put an effort to understand 'This is the path to the end of suffering.'"

(5) "So too, monks, when ghosts pass away, the amount of beings reborn as gods again in their next life is extremely few. However, when ghosts pass away, the amount of beings reborn as animals in their next life is extremely large. What is the reason for this? It is because, monks, they have not understood The Four Noble Truths. What are those Four Noble Truths?

The noble truth of suffering, the noble truth of the cause of suffering, the noble truth of the end of suffering, and the noble truth of the path to the end of suffering."

"Therefore, monks, you must put an effort to understand 'This is suffering.' You must put an effort to understand 'This is the cause of suffering.' You must put an effort to understand 'This is the end of suffering.' You must put an effort to understand 'This is the path to the end of suffering.'"

(6) "So too, monks, when ghosts pass away, the amount of beings reborn as gods again in their next life is extremely few. However, when ghosts pass away, the amount of beings reborn as ghosts in their next life is extremely large. What is the reason for this? It is because, monks, they have not understood The Four Noble Truths. What are those Four Noble Truths?

The noble truth of suffering, the noble truth of the cause of suffering, the noble truth of the end of suffering, and the noble truth of the path to the end of suffering."

"Therefore, monks, you must put an effort to understand 'This is suffering.' You must put an effort to understand 'This is the cause of suffering.' You must put an effort to understand 'This is the end of suffering.' You must put an effort to understand 'This is the path to the end of suffering.'"

This is what the Blessed One taught. With happy minds, those monks delighted in the discourse taught by the Blessed One.

Chapter Four:

Connected Discourses without Discoverable Beginning

4.1 Tinakaṭṭha Suttaṁ—Grass and Wood

This is how I heard. At one time the Blessed One was staying in the province of Sāvatthi, in Jeta's Garden at Anāthapiṇḍika's monastery. The Blessed One addressed the monks, saying, "Oh Monks!" "Bhante!" those monks replied. The Blessed One said thus:

"Monks, this cycle of rebirth is endless. The beginning of this extremely long journey cannot be discovered. These beings, hindered by lack of knowledge of the true nature of life and bound by craving, roam and wander on in this endless journey. Suppose, monks, a person would cut up whatever grass, sticks, branches, and twigs in the entire Indian Sub-Continent and collect them together into a single heap. Then, he cuts them off into four-inch pieces. Then, he would put each piece down, saying for each one 'This is my mother, this is my mother's mother.'

The generation of that person's mothers and grandmothers would not come to an end, yet, the grass, wood, branches, and twigs in this entire Indian Sub-Continent would be used up and finished. What is the reason for that? It is because, monks, this cycle of rebirth is endless. The beginning of this extremely long journey cannot be discovered. These beings, hindered by lack of knowledge of the true nature of life and bound by craving, roam and wander on in this endless journey.

For such a long time, monks, you have experienced various types of suffering, tragedies, and disasters. You have filled the cemetery with your dead bodies. Therefore, monks, the time has come for you to understand the meaningless nature of all conditioned things; the time has come for you to become detached from them; and the time has come for you to be liberated from them."

4.2 Paṭhavi Suttaṁ—The Earth

This is how I heard. At one time, the Blessed One was staying at the province of Sāvatthi, in Jeta's Garden at Anāthapiṇḍika's monastery. The Blessed One addressed the monks, saying, "Oh Monks!" "Bhante!" those monks replied. The Blessed One said thus:

"Monks, this cycle of rebirth is endless. The beginning of this extremely long journey cannot be discovered. These beings, hindered by lack of knowledge of the true nature of life and bound by craving, roam and wander on in this endless journey. Suppose, monks, a person would make clay balls the size of a grape, out of this great earth. Then, he would put each ball down, saying for each one 'This is my father, this is my father's father.'

The generation of that person's fathers and grandfathers would not come to an end, yet, the great earth would be used up and finished. What is the reason for that? It is because, monks, this cycle of rebirth is endless. The beginning of this extremely long journey cannot be discovered. These beings, hindered by lack of knowledge of the true nature of life and bound by craving, roam and wander on in this endless journey.

For such a long time, monks, you have experienced various types of suffering, tragedies, and disasters. You have filled the cemetery with your dead bodies. Therefore, monks, the time has come for you to understand the meaningless nature of all conditioned things; the time has come for you to become detached from them; and the time has come for you to be liberated from them."

4.3 Assu Suttaṁ—Tears

This is how I heard. At one time, the Blessed One was staying at the province of Sāvatthi, in Jeta's Garden at Anāthapiṇḍika's monastery. The Blessed One addressed the monks, saying, "Oh Monks!" "Bhante!" those monks replied. The Blessed One said thus:

"Monks, this cycle of rebirth is endless. The beginning of this extremely long journey cannot be discovered. These beings, hindered by lack of knowledge of the true nature of life and bound by craving, roam and wander on in this endless journey. What do you think, monks, which is more: the stream of tears you have shed as you roamed and wandered on in this journey, crying and weeping because of being united with unfriendly people and unpleasant things, and separated from loved ones and loved belongings—this or the water in the four great oceans?"

"As we understand the Dhamma taught by the Blessed One, Bhante, the stream of tears we have shed as we roamed and wandered on in this journey, crying and weeping because of being united with unfriendly people and unpleasant things, and separated from loved ones and loved belongings—this alone is more than the water in the four great oceans."

"Good, good, monks! It is good that you understand the Dhamma taught by me in such a way. The stream of tears you have shed as you roamed and wandered on in this journey, crying and weeping because of being united with unfriendly people and unpleasant things, and separated from loved ones and loved belongings—this alone is more than the water in the four great oceans. For a long time, monks, you have experienced suffering of the death of your mother; as you have experienced this, crying and weeping because of being united with unfriendly people and unpleasant things, and separated from loved ones and loved belongings, the stream of tears that you have shed is more than the water in the four great oceans."

"For a long time, monks, you have experienced suffering of the death of your father...the death of your brother...the death of your sister...the death of your son...the death of your daughter...the loss of your relatives...the loss of your wealth...the pain of sickness; as you have experienced this, crying and weeping because of being united with unfriendly people and unpleasant things, and separated from loved ones and loved belongings, the stream of tears that you have shed is more than the water in the four great oceans.

"What is the reason for that? It is because, monks, this cycle of rebirth is endless. The beginning of this extremely long journey cannot be discovered. These beings, hindered by lack of knowledge of the true nature of life and bound by craving, roam and wander on in this endless journey."

"For such a long time, monks, you have experienced various types of suffering, tragedies, and disasters. You have filled the cemetery with your dead bodies. Therefore, monks, the time has come for you to understand the meaningless nature of all conditioned things; the time has come for you to become detached from them; and the time has come for you to be liberated from them."

4.4 Mātuthañña Suttaṁ—The Mother's Milk

This is how I heard. At one time, the Blessed One was staying at the province of Sāvatthi, in Jeta's Garden at Anāthapiṇḍika's monastery. The Blessed One addressed the monks, saying, "Oh Monks!" "Bhante!" those monks replied. The Blessed One said thus:

"Monks, this cycle of rebirth is endless. The beginning of this extremely long journey cannot be discovered. These beings, hindered by lack of knowledge of the true nature of life and bound by craving, roam and wander on in this endless journey. What do you think, monks, which is more: the mother's milk that you have drunk as you roamed and wondered on in this long journey—this or the water in the four great oceans?"

"As we understand the Dhamma taught by the Blessed One, Bhante, the mother's milk that we have drunk as we roamed and wandered on in this journey—this alone is more than the water in the four great oceans."

"Good, good, monks! It is good that you understand the Dhamma taught by me in such a way. The mother's milk that you have drunk as you roamed and wandered on in this journey—this alone is more than the water in the four great oceans.

What is the reason for that? It is because, monks, this cycle of rebirth is endless. The beginning of this extremely long journey cannot be discovered. These beings, hindered by lack of knowledge of the true nature of life and bound by craving, roam and wander on in this endless journey.

For such a long time, monks, you have experienced various types of suffering, tragedies, and disasters. You have filled the cemetery with your dead bodies. Therefore, monks, the time has come for you to understand the meaningless nature of all conditioned things; the time has come for you to become detached from them; and the time has come for you to be liberated from them."

4.5 Pabbata Suttaṁ—The Mountain

This is how I heard. At one time, the Blessed One was staying at the province of Sāvatthi, in Jeta's Garden at Anāthapiṇḍika's monastery. A certain monk approached the Blessed One, worshipped Him respectfully and sat down to one side. He asked the Blessed One, "Bhante, how long is an eon?"

"An eon is long, monks. It is not easy to count and say that it is so many years, so many hundreds of years, so many thousands of years, or so many hundreds of thousands of years."

"Then, Bhante, is it possible to give a simile to know the length of an eon?"

"It is possible monks," The Blessed One said. "Suppose, monks, there was a great rocky mountain ten kilometers long, ten kilometers wide, and ten kilometers high, without holes or gaps, and was one solid mass of rock. At the end of every hundred years, a person would stroke it once with a piece of extremely fine Kāsi cloth. By this effort, after a very long time this great rocky mountain might be worn away and eliminated but the eon wouldn't have still come to an end. So long is an eon, monk. It is not just one eon that was passed by, not hundreds of eons, not thousands of eons, and not hundreds of thousands of eons.

What is the reason for that? It is because, monks, this cycle of rebirth is endless. The beginning of this extremely long journey cannot be discovered. These beings, hindered by lack of knowledge of the true nature of life and bound by craving, roam and wander on in this endless journey.

For such a long time, monks, you have experienced various types of suffering, tragedies, and disasters. You have filled the cemetery with your dead bodies. Therefore, monks, the time has come for you to understand the meaningless nature of all conditioned things; the time has come for you to become detached from them; and the time has come for you to be liberated from them."

4.6 Sāsapa Suttaṁ—The Mustard Seeds

This is how I heard. At one time, the Blessed One was staying at the province of Sāvatthi, in Jeta's Garden at Anāthapiṇḍika's monastery. A certain monk approached the Blessed One, worshipped Him respectfully and sat down to one side. He asked the Blessed One, "Bhante, how long is an eon?"

"An eon is long, monks. It is not easy to count and say that it is so many years, so many hundreds of years, so many thousands of years, or so many hundreds of thousands of years."

"Then, Bhante, is it possible to give a simile to know the length of an eon?"

"It is possible monks," The Blessed One said. "Suppose, monks, there was a city with iron walls ten kilometers long, ten kilometers wide, and ten kilometers high, filled with mustard seeds. At the end of every hundred years, a person would take away one mustard seed from there. As a result of this, the great heap of mustard seeds might be soon taken away, but the eon wouldn't have still come to an end. So long is an eon, monk. It is not just one eon that was passed by, not hundreds of eons, not thousands of eons, and not hundreds of thousands of eons.

What is the reason for that? It is because, monks, this cycle of rebirth is endless. The beginning of this extremely long journey cannot be discovered. These beings, hindered by lack of knowledge of the true nature of life and bound by craving, roam and wander on in this endless journey.

For such a long time, monks, you have experienced various types of suffering, tragedies, and disasters. You have filled the cemetery with your dead bodies. Therefore, monks, the time has come for you to understand the meaningless nature of all conditioned things; the time has come for you to become detached from them; and the time has come for you to be liberated from them."

4.7 Sāvaka Suttaṁ—The Disciple

This is how I heard. At one time, the Blessed One was staying at the province of Sāvatthi, in Jeta's Garden at Anāthapiṇḍika's monastery. A number of monks approached the Blessed One, worshipped Him respectfully and sat down to one side. They asked the Blessed One, "Bhante, how many eons have passed by and gone by?"

"Monks many eons have passed by and gone by. It is not easy to count them and say there are so many eons, so many hundreds of eons, so many thousands of eons, or so many hundreds of thousands of eons."

"Then, Bhante, is it possible to give a simile to know how many eons have passed by and gone by?"

"It is possible, monks," The Blessed One said. "Suppose, monks, there were four disciples near me each with a life span of a hundred years, living a hundred years and each day they were each to recollect a hundred thousand eons. There would still be eons not yet recollected by them. But those four disciples, each with a life span of a hundred years, living a hundred years, would pass away at the end of a hundred years. It is not easy to count them and say that there are so many eons, or so many hundreds of eons, or so many thousands of eons, or so many hundreds of thousands of eons.

What is the reason for that? It is because, monks, this cycle of rebirth is endless. The beginning of this extremely long journey cannot be discovered. These beings, hindered by lack of knowledge of the true nature of life and bound by craving, roam and wander on in this endless journey.

For such a long time, monks, you have experienced various types of suffering, tragedies, and disasters. You have filled the cemetery with your dead bodies. Therefore, monks, the time has come for you to understand the meaningless nature of all conditioned things; the time has come for you to become detached from them; and the time has come for you to be liberated from them."

4.8 Gaṁgā Suttaṁ—The River Gaṁgā

This is how I heard. At one time, the Blessed One was staying at the city of Rājagaha, in the Bamboo Garden, at the Squirrel Park. Then, a certain brāhmin approached the Blessed One, and exchanged greetings with him. After their greetings and friendly talk, the brāhmin sat down to one side and said to the Buddha, "Master Gotama, how many eons have passed by and gone by?"

"Brāhmin, many eons have passed by and gone by. It is not easy to count them and say there are so many eons, or so many hundreds of eons, or so many thousands of eons, or so many hundreds of thousands of eons."

"But, Master Gotama, is it possible to give a simile to know how many eons have passed by and gone by?"

"It is possible, brāhmin," The Blessed One said, "Brāhmin, let us think about the amount of grains of sand between the point where the river Gaṁgā starts and the point where it enters the great ocean. It is not easy to count them and say there are so many grains of sand, so many hundreds of grains, so many thousands of grains, or so many hundreds of thousands of grains.

Brāhmin, the amount of eons that have passed by and gone by are even greater than that. It is not easy to count them and say that there are so many eons, so many hundreds of eons, so many thousands of eons, or so many hundreds of thousands of eons. What is the reason for that? It is because, brāhmin, this cycle of rebirth is endless. The beginning of this extremely long journey cannot be discovered. These beings, hindered by lack of knowledge of the true nature of life and bound by craving, roam and wander on in this endless journey.

For such a long time, brāhmin, you have experienced various types of suffering, tragedies, and disasters. You have filled the cemetery with your dead bodies. Therefore, brāhmin, the time has come for you to understand the meaningless nature of all conditioned things; the time has come for you to become detached from them; and the time has come for you to be liberated from them."

When the Buddha taught this discourse, that brāhmin said to the Blessed One, "It is wonderful, Master Gotama! It is excellent, Master Gotama! Just as a man were to set upright what was overturned, to reveal what was hidden, to show the way to one who was lost, or to carry a lamp into the dark so that those with eyes could see forms, in the same way, the Dhamma has been made clear in many ways by the Master Gotama. I go for refuge to the Master Gotama, to the Dhamma, and to the community of monks. Master Gotama, from today, please accept me as a lay follower who has gone for refuge to Buddha, Dhamma, and Sangha until my life lasts."

4.9 Daṇḍa Suttaṁ—The Stick

This is how I heard. At one time, the Blessed One was staying at the province of Sāvatthi, in Jeta's Garden at Anāthapiṇḍika's monastery. The Blessed One addressed the monks, saying, "Oh Monks!" "Bhante!" those monks replied. The Blessed One said thus:

"Monks, this cycle of rebirth is endless. The beginning of this extremely long journey cannot be discovered. These beings, hindered by lack of knowledge of the true nature of life and bound by craving, roam and wander on in this endless journey.

Monks, if someone were to throw a stick up into the air it would fall on its bottom at one time, another time it would fall on its side, and still another time it would fall on its top. In the same way, monks, beings hindered by lack of knowledge of the true nature of life and bound by craving, roam and wonder on in this long journey of rebirths, go from this world to the next world and another time they come from the other world to this world.

What is the reason for that? It is because, monks, this cycle of rebirth is endless. The beginning of this extremely long journey cannot be discovered. These beings, hindered by lack of knowledge of the true nature of life and bound by craving, roam and wander on in this endless journey.

For such a long time, monks, you have experienced various types of suffering, tragedies, and disasters. You have filled the cemetery with your dead bodies. Therefore, monks, the time has come for you to understand the meaningless nature of all conditioned things; the time has come for you to become detached from them; and the time has come for you to be liberated from them."

4.10 Eka Puggala Suttaṁ—Single Person

At one time, the Blessed One was staying in the city of Rājagaha on the Gijjhakūta Mountain. The Blessed One addressed the monks, saying, "Oh Monks!" "Bhante!" those monks replied. The Blessed One said thus:

"Monks, this cycle of rebirth is endless. The beginning of this extremely long journey cannot be discovered. These beings, hindered by lack of knowledge of the true nature of life and bound by craving, roam and wander on in this endless journey. Monks, if there was someone to collect the skeletons of a single person who roams and wanders on through one eon and if what was collected would not get destroyed, then there would be a stack of bones, a pile of bones, a heap of bones as large as this Vepulla mountain.

What is the reason for that? It is because, monks, this cycle of rebirth is endless. The beginning of this extremely long journey cannot be discovered. These beings, hindered by lack of knowledge of the true nature of life and bound by craving, roam and wander on in this endless journey.

For such a long time, monks, you have experienced various types of suffering, tragedies, and disasters. You have filled the cemetery with your dead bodies. Therefore, monks, the time has come for you to understand the meaningless nature of all conditioned things; the time has come for you to become detached from them; and the time has come for you to be liberated from them."

The Blessed One taught this discourse. Having taught this, the Well Gone One, the Great Teacher, further said thus:

"The Great Sage, the Buddha, said that the heap of bones collected of a single person wandering through a single eon would make a heap as high as Vepulla Mountain.

The massive Vepulla Mountain is standing north of Gijjhakūta Mountain in the Magadhan mountain range.

When a noble disciple understands suffering, the cause of suffering, the overcoming of suffering, and the Noble

Eightfold Path that leads to the end of suffering, having wandered on in this journey of rebirths for seven more times at most, he will make an end to suffering by destroying all the fetters of defilements."

4.11 Duggata Suttaṁ—The Poor Person

This is how I heard. At one time, the Blessed One was staying at the province of Sāvatthi, in Jeta's Garden at Anāthapiṇḍika's monastery. The Blessed One addressed the monks, saying, "Oh Monks!" "Bhante!" those monks replied. The Blessed One said thus:

"Monks, this cycle of rebirth is endless. The beginning of this extremely long journey cannot be discovered. These beings, hindered by lack of knowledge of the true nature of life and bound by craving, roam and wander on in this endless journey. Monks, whenever you see anyone ugly, very poor, and depressed, you can conclude, 'We too have suffered in the exact same way, many times in this long journey."

"What is the reason for that? It is because, monks, this cycle of rebirth is endless. The beginning of this extremely long journey cannot be discovered. These beings, hindered by lack of knowledge of the true nature of life and bound by craving, roam and wander on in this endless journey."

"For such a long time, monks, you have experienced various types of suffering, tragedies, and disasters. You have filled the cemetery with your dead bodies. Therefore, monks, the time has come for you to understand the meaningless nature of all conditioned things; the time has come for you to become detached from them; and the time has come for you to be liberated from them."

4.12 Sukhita Suttaṁ—The Happy Person

This is how I heard. At one time, the Blessed One was staying at the province of Sāvatthi, in Jeta's Garden at Anāthapiṇḍika's monastery. The Blessed One addressed the monks, saying, "Oh Monks!" "Bhante!" those monks replied. The Blessed One said thus:

"Monks, this cycle of rebirth is endless. The beginning of this extremely long journey cannot be discovered. These beings, hindered by lack of knowledge of the true nature of life and bound by craving, roam and wander on in this endless journey. Monks, whenever you see anyone beautiful, very rich, and happy, you can conclude, 'We too have enjoyed comforts in the exact same way, many times in this long journey.'

What is the reason for that? It is because, monks, this cycle of rebirth is endless. The beginning of this extremely long journey cannot be discovered. These beings, hindered by lack of knowledge of the true nature of life and bound by craving, roam and wander on in this endless journey."

"For such a long time, monks, you have experienced various types of suffering, tragedies, and disasters. You have filled the cemetery with your dead bodies. Therefore, monks, the time has come for you to understand the meaningless nature of all conditioned things; the time has come for you to become detached from them; and the time has come for you to be liberated from them."

4.13 Tiṁsamatta Suttaṁ—Around Thirty Monks

At one time, the Blessed One was staying at the city of Rājagaha, in the Bamboo Garden, at the Squirrel Park. In the province of Pāvā, there lived about thirty monks. All of them were forest dwellers, almsfood eaters, rag-robe wearers, and triple-robe users. Yet, they were all still with fetters of defilements.

One day, they all approached the Blessed One, worshipped him and sat down to one side. Then it occurred to the Blessed One, "These thirty monks live in the province of Pāvā. All of them are forest dwellers, almsfood eaters, rag-robe wearers and triple-robe users. Yet, they are all still with fetters of defilements. Let me teach them the Dhamma in such a way that their minds will be liberated from taints through non-clinging while they are sitting in these very seats."

Then, the Blessed One addressed those monks, "Oh, monks!" "Bhante!" those monks replied. The Blessed One asked, "Monks, this cycle of rebirth is endless. The beginning of this extremely long journey cannot be discovered. These beings, hindered by lack of knowledge of the true nature of life and bound by craving, roam and wander on in this endless journey. What do you think, monks, which is more: the stream of blood you have shed when you were beheaded as you roamed and wandered on in this journey—this or the water in the four great oceans?"

"As we understand the Dhamma taught by the Blessed One, Bhante, the stream of blood that we have shed when we were beheaded as we roamed and wandered on in this journey—this alone is more than the water in the four great oceans."

"Good, good, monks! It is good that you understand the Dhamma taught by me in such a way. The stream of blood that you have shed when you were beheaded as you roamed and wandered on in this journey—this alone is more than the water in the four great oceans. For a long time, monks, you have been cows and when beheaded as cows, the stream of blood that you shed is greater than the water in the four great oceans.

For a long time, monks, you have been buffalo... sheep... goats... deer... chickens... and pigs; and when beheaded as pigs, the stream of blood that you shed is greater than the water in the four great oceans.

For a long time, monks, you have been arrested as burglars... as highwaymen... and as men who engaged in sexual misconduct; and when you were beheaded, the stream of blood that you shed is greater than the water in the four great oceans.

What is the reason for that? It is because, monks, this cycle of rebirth is endless. The beginning of this extremely long journey cannot be discovered. These beings, hindered by lack of knowledge of the true nature of life and bound by craving, roam and wander on in this endless journey.

For such a long time, monks, you have experienced various types of suffering, tragedies, and disasters. You have filled the cemetery with your dead bodies. Therefore, monks, the time has come for you to understand the meaningless nature of all conditioned things; the time has come for you to become detached from them; and the time has come for you to be liberated from them."

The Blessed One taught this discourse. Those monks rejoiced and delighted in the Blessed One's discourse. While this Dhamma was being taught, the minds of the thirty monks from the province of Pāvā were liberated from the taints through non-clinging.

4.14 Mātu Suttaṁ—Mother

This is how I heard. At one time, the Blessed One was staying at the province of Sāvatthi, in Jeta's Garden at Anāthapiṇḍika's monastery. The Blessed One addressed the monks, saying, "Oh Monks!" "Bhante!" those monks replied. The Blessed One said thus:

"Monks, this cycle of rebirth is endless. The beginning of this extremely long journey cannot be discovered. These beings, hindered by lack of knowledge of the true nature of life and bound by craving, roam and wander on in this endless journey. Monks, in this long journey, it is not easy to find a being who has not previously been a mother.

What is the reason for that? It is because, monks, this cycle of rebirth is endless. The beginning of this extremely long journey cannot be discovered. These beings, hindered by lack of knowledge of the true nature of life and bound by craving, roam and wander on in this endless journey.

For such a long time, monks, you have experienced various types of suffering, tragedies, and disasters. You have filled the cemetery with your dead bodies. Therefore, monks, the time has come for you to understand the meaningless nature of all conditioned things; the time has come for you to become detached from them; and the time has come for you to be liberated from them."

4.15 Pitu Suttaṁ—Father

This is how I heard. At one time, the Blessed One was staying at the province of Sāvatthi, in Jeta's Garden at Anāthapiṇḍika's monastery. The Blessed One addressed the monks, saying, "Oh Monks!" "Bhante!" those monks replied. The Blessed One said thus:

"Monks, this cycle of rebirth is endless. The beginning of this extremely long journey cannot be discovered. These beings, hindered by lack of knowledge of the true nature of life and bound by craving, roam and wander on in this endless journey. Monks, in this long journey, it is not easy to find a being who has not previously been a father.

What is the reason for that? It is because, monks, this cycle of rebirth is endless. The beginning of this extremely long journey cannot be discovered. These beings, hindered by lack of knowledge of the true nature of life and bound by craving, roam and wander on in this endless journey.

For such a long time, monks, you have experienced various types of suffering, tragedies, and disasters. You have filled the cemetery with your dead bodies. Therefore, monks, the time has come for you to understand the meaningless nature of all conditioned things; the time has come for you to become detached from them; and the time has come for you to be liberated from them."

4.16 Bhātu Suttaṁ—Brother

This is how I heard. At one time, the Blessed One was staying at the province of Sāvatthi, in Jeta's Garden at Anāthapiṇḍika's monastery. The Blessed One addressed the monks, saying, "Oh Monks!" "Bhante!" those monks replied. The Blessed One said thus:

"Monks, this cycle of rebirth is endless. The beginning of this extremely long journey cannot be discovered. These beings, hindered by lack of knowledge of the true nature of life and bound by craving, roam and wander on in this endless journey. Monks, in this long journey, it is not easy to find a being who has not previously been a brother.

What is the reason for that? It is because, monks, this cycle of rebirth is endless. The beginning of this extremely long journey cannot be discovered. These beings, hindered by lack of knowledge of the true nature of life and bound by craving, roam and wander on in this endless journey.

For such a long time, monks, you have experienced various types of suffering, tragedies, and disasters. You have filled the cemetery with your dead bodies. Therefore, monks, the time has come for you to understand the meaningless nature of all conditioned things; the time has come for you to become detached from them; and the time has come for you to be liberated from them."

4.17 Bhagini Suttaṁ—Sister

This is how I heard. At one time, the Blessed One was staying at the province of Sāvatthi, in Jeta's Garden at Anāthapiṇḍika's monastery. The Blessed One addressed the monks, saying, "Oh Monks!" "Bhante!" those monks replied. The Blessed One said thus:

"Monks, this cycle of rebirth is endless. The beginning of this extremely long journey cannot be discovered. These beings, hindered by lack of knowledge of the true nature of life and bound by craving, roam and wander on in this endless journey. Monks, in this long journey, it is not easy to find a being who has not previously been a sister.

What is the reason for that? It is because, monks, this cycle of rebirth is endless. The beginning of this extremely long journey cannot be discovered. These beings, hindered by lack of knowledge of the true nature of life and bound by craving, roam and wander on in this endless journey.

For such a long time, monks, you have experienced various types of suffering, tragedies, and disasters. You have filled the cemetery with your dead bodies. Therefore, monks, the time has come for you to understand the meaningless nature of all conditioned things; the time has come for you to become detached from them; and the time has come for you to be liberated from them."

4.18 Putta Suttaṁ—Son

This is how I heard. At one time, the Blessed One was staying at the province of Sāvatthi, in Jeta's Garden at Anāthapiṇḍika's monastery. The Blessed One addressed the monks, saying, "Oh Monks!" "Bhante!" those monks replied. The Blessed One said thus:

"Monks, this cycle of rebirth is endless. The beginning of this extremely long journey cannot be discovered. These beings, hindered by lack of knowledge of the true nature of life and bound by craving, roam and wander on in this endless journey. Monks, in this long journey, it is not easy to find a being who has not previously been a son.

What is the reason for that? It is because, monks, this cycle of rebirth is endless. The beginning of this extremely long journey cannot be discovered. These beings, hindered by lack of knowledge of the true nature of life and bound by craving, roam and wander on in this endless journey.

For such a long time, monks, you have experienced various types of suffering, tragedies, and disasters. You have filled the cemetery with your dead bodies. Therefore, monks, the time has come for you to understand the meaningless nature of all conditioned things; the time has come for you to become detached from them; and the time has come for you to be liberated from them."

4.19 Dhītu Suttaṁ—Daughter

This is how I heard. At one time, the Blessed One was staying at the province of Sāvatthi, in Jeta's Garden at Anāthapiṇḍika's monastery. The Blessed One addressed the monks, saying, "Oh Monks!" "Bhante!" those monks replied. The Blessed One said thus:

"Monks, this cycle of rebirth is endless. The beginning of this extremely long journey cannot be discovered. These beings, hindered by lack of knowledge of the true nature of life and bound by craving, roam and wander on in this endless journey. Monks, in this long journey, it is not easy to find a being who has not previously been a daughter.

What is the reason for that? It is because, monks, this cycle of rebirth is endless. The beginning of this extremely long journey cannot be discovered. These beings, hindered by lack of knowledge of the true nature of life and bound by craving, roam and wander on in this endless journey.

For such a long time, monks, you have experienced various types of suffering, tragedies, and disasters. You have filled the cemetery with your dead bodies. Therefore, monks, the time has come for you to understand the meaningless nature of all conditioned things; the time has come for you to become detached from them; and the time has come for you to be liberated from them."

4.20 Vēpulla Suttaṁ—Vēpulla Mountain

At one time, the Blessed One was staying in the city of Rājagaha on the Gijjhakūta Mountain. The Blessed One addressed the monks, saying, "Oh Monks!" "Bhante!" those monks replied. The Blessed One said thus:

"Monks, this cycle of rebirth is endless. The beginning of this extremely long journey cannot be discovered. These beings, hindered by lack of knowledge of the true nature of life and bound by craving, roam and wander on in this endless journey.

Monks, in the past, this Vēpulla mountain was called Pācinavaṁsa and the people who lived at that time were called Tivaras. The lifespan of Tivaras was 40,000 years. They could climb the Pācinavaṁsa mountain in four days and descend in four days. At that time, the Blessed One Kakusandha, the Arahant, the supremely enlightened Buddha lived in the world. Monk Vidhura and monk Sañjīva were his two chief disciples. See, monks! The previous name for this mountain has disappeared, those people have died, and that Blessed One has passed away. So impermanent are conditioned things, monks, so unstable, so unreliable. Therefore, monks, the time has come for you to understand the meaningless nature of all conditioned things; the time has come for you to become detached from them; and the time has come for you to be liberated from them."

"At another time, monks, in the past, this Vēpulla mountain was called Vaṇkaka and the people who lived at that time were called Rohitassas. The lifespan of Rohitassas was 30,000 years. They could climb the Vaṇkaka mountain in three days and descend in three days. At that time, the Blessed One Koṇāgamana, the Arahant, the supremely enlightened Buddha lived in the world. Monk Bhiyyosa and monk Uttara were his two chief disciples. See, monks! The previous name for this mountain has disappeared, those people have died, and that Blessed One has passed away. So impermanent are conditioned things, monks, so unstable, so unreliable. Therefore, monks, the time has come for you to understand the meaningless nature of all conditioned things; the time has come for you to become detached from them; and the time has come for you to be liberated from them."

"At still another time, monks, in the past, this Vēpulla mountain was called Supassa and the people who lived at that time were called Suppiyas. The lifespan of Suppiyas was 20,000 years. They could climb the Supassa mountain in two days and descend in two days. At that time, the Blessed One Kassapa, the Arahant, the supremely enlightened Buddha lived in the world. Monk Tissa and monk Bhāradvāja were his two chief disciples. See, monks! The previous name for this mountain has disappeared, those people have died, and that Blessed One has passed away. So impermanent are conditioned things, monks, so unstable, so unreliable. Therefore, monks, the time has come for you to understand the meaningless nature of all conditioned things; the time has come for you to become detached from them; and the time has come for you to be liberated from them."

"At present, monks, this Vēpulla mountain is called Vēpulla and at present these people are called Magadhans. The lifespan of Magadhans is short, limited, and passing quickly; one who lives long, lives a hundred years, or a little more. The Magadhans climb the Vēpulla mountain in a moment and descend in a moment. At present, I live in the world, the Arahant, the supremely enlightened one. Monk Sāriputta and monk Moggallāna are my two chief disciples. There will come a time, monks, when the name for this mountain will have disappeared, when these people will have died, and I will have passed away. So impermanent are conditioned things, monks, so unstable, so unreliable. Therefore, monks, the time has come for you to understand the meaningless nature of all conditioned things; the time has come for you to become detached from them; and the time has come for you to be liberated from them."

The Blessed One taught this. Having taught this, the Well Gone One, the Great Teacher, further said thus:

"The mountain Vepulla was called Pācīnavaṁsa by the Tivaras, Vaṇkaka by the Rohitassas, Supassa by the Suppiyas, and Vepulla by the Magadhans.

Conditioned things are indeed impermanent, their nature is to arise and pass away. Having arisen, they cease: the cessation of desire for all conditioned things is truly the ultimate bliss."

Chapter Five:

Goal of Human Life

5.1 Chiggala Suttam—Hole

"Monks, suppose a person would throw a piece of wood with a single hole in it into the great ocean. There was a blind turtle in that great ocean. It would come to the surface once every hundred years. What do you think, monks, would that blind turtle coming to the surface only every hundred years, insert its neck into that hole of the wood piece?"

"If it would ever do so, Bhante, it would be only after a very long time."

"Monks, that blind turtle coming to the surface once every hundred years, would insert its neck into the hole of the wooden piece sooner, I say. However, the regaining of the human life of a foolish person who has been reborn just once in the plane of misery is even harder. What is the reason for this? Monks, in the plane of misery, there is not any practise of the Dhamma or any making of merit. Monks, in the plane of misery, there is this mutual devouring, the devouring of the weak."

"What is the reason for that? Monks, these beings have not realised The Four Noble Truths. What are these four noble truths? The noble truth of suffering, the noble truth of the cause of suffering, the noble truth of the end of suffering, and the noble truth of the path to end suffering."

"Therefore, monks, you must put an effort to understand: 'This is suffering.' You must put an effort to understand:

'This is the cause of suffering.' You must put an effort to understand: 'This is the end of suffering.' You must put an effort to understand: 'This is the path to end suffering."

5.2 Chiggala Suttaṁ—Hole (2)

"Monks, suppose that this great earth had become one mass of water. A person would throw a piece of wood with a single hole in it. The wind coming from the east, carries the piece of wood towards the west; the wind coming from the west, carries the piece of wood towards the east; the wind coming from the north, carries the piece of wood towards the south; and the wind coming from the south, carries the piece of wood towards the north. Suppose there was a blind turtle in that great body of water. It would come to the surface once every hundred years. What do you think, monks, would that blind turtle coming to the surface only every hundred years, insert its neck into that hole of the wood piece?"

"Bhante, it would be after a very long time, extremely rare, that the blind turtle, coming to the surface once every hundred years, insert its neck into the hole of the wooden piece".

"In the same way, monks, it is after a very long time, extremely rare, that a being is born as a human; it is after a very long time, extremely rare, that the Tathāgata, the Arahant, the supremely enlightened Buddha is born into the world; and it is after a very long time, extremely rare, that the teachings and the discipline preached by the Buddha shine in the world."

"Monks, you have obtained that extremely rare human life; the Tathāgata, the Arahant, the supremely enlightened Buddha has been born into the world; and the teachings and discipline preached by the Buddha shine in the world."

"Therefore, monks, you must put an effort to understand: 'This is suffering.' You must put an effort to understand: 'This is the cause of suffering.' You must put an effort to understand: 'This is the end of suffering.' You must put an effort to understand: 'This is the path to end suffering.'"

5.3 Sattisata Suttaṁ—A Hundred Spears

"Monks, suppose there were a person with a life span of a hundred years. Someone would say to him: 'Come, man, in the morning my people will strike you with a hundred spears; at noon they will strike you with a hundred spears; and in the evening they will strike you with a hundred spears. In this way, being struck day after day by three hundred spears you still, will have a life span of a hundred years, and will live a hundred years; and then, after a hundred years have passed, you will be able to realise The Four Noble Truths which you have not realised before.'"

"Monks, it is fitting for a son or a daughter who understands the benefit of realising the truth to enter the Buddha's path and to become a monk or a nun. What is the reason for this? Monks, this cycle of rebirth is endless. If one were to see for how many times one has been stroke by spears, swords, and axes in this cycle, one is unable to discover the beginning of this extremely long journey."

"Monks, even though this may be so, I do not say that one should realise The Four Noble Truths with such severe pain and grief. Rather, I say that one can realise The Four Noble Truths with joy and happiness. What are these Four Noble Truths? The noble truth of suffering, the noble truth of the cause of suffering, the noble truth of the end of suffering, and the noble truth of the path to end suffering."

"Therefore, monks, you must put an effort to understand: 'This is suffering.' You must put an effort to understand: 'This is the cause of suffering.' You must put an effort to understand: 'This is the end of suffering.' You must put an effort to understand: 'This is the path to end suffering.'"

5.4 Pāna Suttaṁ—Creatures

"Monks, suppose a person were to cut up whatever grass, sticks, branches, and twigs there is in this Indian Sub-Continent and collect them into a single pile. Having done so, he would sharpen them into arrow-like sticks. Then, he would pierce the large creatures in the ocean with large sharp sticks. He would pierce the middle-sized creatures in the ocean with middle-sized sharp sticks. He would pierce the small creatures in the ocean with small sharp sticks. Still, monks, he would not have pierced all big and visible creatures in the ocean even after all the grass, sticks, branches and twigs in the Indian Sub-Continent would have been used up and finished. Monks, the small creatures in the ocean that could not easily be pierced by sharp sticks would be even more numerous than big and visible creatures. What is the reason for that? Monks, the reason is the subtleness of lives and the vastness of the plane of misery."

"Monks, the disciple who possesses right view and understands The Four Noble Truths as they really are, 'this is suffering, this is the cause of suffering, this is the end of suffering, and this is the path to end suffering', is freed from that vast plane of misery."

"Therefore, monks, you must put an effort to understand: 'This is suffering.' You must put an effort to understand: 'This is the cause of suffering.' You must put an effort to understand: 'This is the end of suffering.' You must put an effort to understand: 'This is the path to end suffering.'"

5.5 Cela Suttaṁ—Clothes on Fire

"Monks, if one's clothes or head caught fire, what should he or she do about it?" "Bhante, if ones clothes or head caught fire, he or she must arouse extraordinary desire, make an extraordinary effort, and act with extraordinary willingness, eagerness, enthusiasm, mindfulness, and wise awareness to extinguish the fire."

"Monks, paying no attention to that fire and being equanimous at it that person must arouse extraordinary desire, make an extraordinary effort, and act with extraordinary willingness, eagerness, enthusiasm, mindfulness, and wise awareness to realise as they really are, The Four Noble Truths that have not yet been realised. What are these Four Noble Truths? The noble truth of suffering, the noble truth of the cause of suffering, the noble truth of the end of suffering, and the noble truth of the path to end suffering."

"Therefore, monks, you must put an effort to understand: 'This is suffering'. You must put an effort to understand: 'This is the cause of suffering'. You must put an effort to understand: 'This is the end of suffering'. You must put an effort to understand: 'This is the path to end suffering.'"

5.6 Papata Suttaṁ—Steep Cliff

At one time, the Blessed One was staying in the city of Rājagaha on the Gijjhakūta Mountain. Then, the Blessed One addressed the monks saying, "Come, monks, let us go to the Paṭibhāna mountain peak for spending the afternoon."

"Yes, Bhante," replied those monks. Then, the Blessed One, together with a number of monks, went to the Paṭibhāna Mountain peak. There, a certain monk saw the steep cliff of the Paṭibhāna mountain peak and asked the Blessed One, "Bhante, this cliff is indeed steep. Bhante, this cliff is indeed extremely steep. Bhante, is there any other cliff steeper and more frightful than this one?"

"Monk, there is another cliff steeper and more frightful than this one."

"Bhante, what is that cliff that is steeper and more frightful than this one?"

"Monk, some people do not understand The Four Noble Truths as they really are, 'this is suffering, this is the cause of suffering, this is the end of suffering, and this is the path to end suffering'. As a result, they crave for the formations that lead to birth, the formations that lead to aging, the formations that lead to death, and the formations that lead to sorrow, weeping, pain, depression, and sighing."

"Having craved for the formations that lead to birth, aging, death, sorrow, weeping, pain, depression, and sighing, they generate the formations that lead to birth, aging, death, sorrow, weeping, pain, depression, and sighing. Having generated such formations, they tumble down the cliff of birth, the cliff of aging, the cliff of death, and the cliff of sorrow, weeping, pain, depression, and sighing. They are not freed from birth, aging, death, sorrow, weeping, pain, depression, and sighing, I say."

"However, monks, some people do understand The Four Noble Truths as they really are, 'this is suffering, this is the cause of suffering, this is the end of suffering, and this is the path to end suffering.' As a result, they do not crave for the formations that lead to birth, the formations that lead to aging, the formations that lead to death, and the formations that lead to sorrow, weeping, pain, depression, and sighing."

"Having not craved for the formations that lead to birth, aging, death, sorrow, weeping, pain, depression, and sighing, they do not generate the formations that lead to birth, aging, death, sorrow, weeping, pain, depression, and sighing. Having not generated such formations, they do not tumble down the cliff of birth, the cliff of aging, the cliff of death, and the cliff of sorrow, weeping, pain, depression, and sighing. They are freed from birth, aging, death, sorrow, weeping, pain, depression, and sighing, I say."

"Therefore, monks, you must put an effort to understand: 'This is suffering.' You must put an effort to understand: 'This is the cause of suffering.' You must put an effort to understand: 'This is the end of suffering.' You must put an effort to understand: 'This is the path to end suffering.'"

5.7 Parilāha Suttaṁ—Parilāha Hell

"Monks, there is a hell called Great Parilāha. There, whatever form one sees with the eye is undesirable, never desirable; unlovely, never lovely; and unpleasant, never pleasant. Whatever sound one hears with the ear... Whatever odour one smells with the nose... Whatever flavour one tastes with the tongue... Whatever tangible object one feels with the body... What ever thought one experiences with the mind is undesirable, never desirable; unlovely, never lovely; and unpleasant, never pleasant."

When the Blessed One told this, a certain monk asked the Buddha: "Bhante, that Great Parilā Hell is indeed terrible. Bhante, that Great Parilā Hell is indeed extremely terrible. However, Bhante, is there any other Hell more terrible and frightful than that one?"

"Monk, there is another Hell more terrible and frightful than that one."

"Bhante, what is that Hell that is more terrible and frightful than Great Parilāha Hell?"

"Monk, some people do not understand The Four Noble Truths as they really are, 'this is suffering, this is the cause of suffering, this is the end of suffering, and this is the path to end suffering.' As a result, they crave for the formations that lead to birth, the formations that lead to aging, the formations that lead to death, and the formations that lead to sorrow, weeping, pain, depression, and sighing."

"Having craved for the formations that lead to birth, aging, death, sorrow, weeping, pain, depression, and sighing, they generate the formations that lead to birth, aging, death, sorrow, weeping, pain, depression, and sighing. Having generated such formations, they are burnt by the Hell of birth, the Hell of aging, the Hell of death, and the Hell of sorrow, weeping, pain, depression, and sighing. They are not freed from birth, aging, death, sorrow, weeping, pain, depression, and sighing, I say."

"However, monks, some people do understand The Four Noble Truths as they really are, 'this is suffering, this is the cause of suffering, this is the end of suffering, and this is the path to end suffering'. As a result, they do not crave for the formations that lead to birth, the formations that lead to aging, the formations that lead to death, and the formations that lead to sorrow, weeping, pain, depression, and sighing."

"Having not craved for the formations that lead to birth, aging, death, sorrow, weeping, pain, depression, and sighing, they do not generate the formations that lead to birth, aging, death, sorrow, weeping, pain, depression, and sighing. Having not generated such formations, they are not burnt by the Hell of birth, the Hell of aging, the Hell of death, and the Hell of sorrow, weeping, pain, depression, and sighing. They are freed from birth, aging, death, sorrow, weeping, pain, depression, and sighing, I say."

"Therefore, monks, you must put an effort to understand: 'This is suffering.' You must put an effort to understand: 'This is the cause of suffering.' You must put an effort to understand: 'This is the end of suffering.' You must put an effort to understand: 'This is the path to end suffering."

5.8 Andhakāra Suttaṁ—Darkness

"Monks, there is an empty space in this world that is of blinding dense darkness, where, even so powerful and mighty sunlight or moonlight does not reach."

When the Blessed One told this, a certain monk asked the Buddha: "Bhante, the darkness is indeed great; Bhante, the darkness is indeed extremely great. However, Bhante, is there any darkness greater and more frightful than this one?"

"Monks, there is another Darkness that is greater and more frightful than this one."

"Bhante, what is that Darkness that is greater and more frightful than this Darkness?"

"Monks, some people do not understand The Four Noble Truths as they really are, 'this is suffering, this is the cause of suffering, this is the end of suffering, and this is the path to end suffering.' As a result, they crave for the formations that lead to birth, the formations that lead to aging, the formations that lead to death, and the formations that lead to sorrow, weeping, pain, depression, and sighing."

"Having craved for the formations that lead to birth, aging, death, sorrow, weeping, pain, depression, and sighing, they generate the formations that lead to birth, aging, death, sorrow, weeping, pain, depression, and sighing. Having generated such formations, they tumble into the darkness of birth, the darkness of aging, the darkness of death, and the darkness of sorrow, weeping, pain, depression, and sighing. They are not freed from birth, aging, death, sorrow, weeping, pain, depression, and sighing, I say."

"However, monks, some people do understand The Four Noble Truths as they really are, 'this is suffering, this is the cause of suffering, this is the end of suffering, and this is the path to end suffering.' As a result, they do not crave for the formations that lead to birth, the formations that lead to aging, the formations that lead to death, and the formations that lead to sorrow, weeping, pain, depression, and sighing."

"Having not craved for the formations that lead to birth, aging, death, sorrow, weeping, pain, depression, and sighing, they do not generate the formations that lead to birth, aging, death, sorrow, weeping, pain, depression, and sighing. Having not generated such formations, they do not tumble into the darkness of birth, the darkness of aging, the darkness of death, and the darkness of sorrow, weeping, pain, depression, and sighing. They are freed from birth, aging, death, sorrow, weeping, pain, depression, and sighing, I say."

"Therefore, monks, you must put an effort to understand: 'This is suffering.' You must put an effort to understand: 'This is the cause of suffering.' You must put an effort to understand: 'This is the end of suffering.' You must put an effort to understand: 'This is the path to end suffering.'"

Mahamegha English Publications:

Sutta Translations

Stories of Sakka, Lords of Gods: Sakka Samyutta

Stories of Brahmas: Brahma Samyutta

Stories of Heavenly Mansions: Vimanavatthu

Stories of Ghosts: Petavatthu

The Voice of Enlightened Monks: The Theragatha

The Voice of Enlightened Nuns: The Therigatha

What does the Buddha really teach? (Dhammapada)

Dhamma Books

Mahamevnawa Pali-English Paritta Chanting Book

The Wise Shall Realize

The Life of the Buddha for Children

Children's Picture Books

Chaththa Manawaka

Sumana the Novice Monk

Stingy Kosiya of Town Sakkara

Kisagothami

Kali the She-Devil

Ayuwaddana Kumaraya

Sumana the Florist

Sirigutta and Garahadinna

The Banker Anathapindika